FROM THE LIBRARY OF
Lucy McMullen
READ IT - LOVE IT - RETURN IT

A collection of enlightened musings

Heart Notes

K P WEAVER

Published by

Copyright © 2020 Karen Weaver

All rights reserved. No part of this book may be used or reproduced by any means, graphic, electronic, or mechanical, including photocopying, recording, taping or by any information storage retrieval system without the written permission of the copyright owner except in the case of brief quotations embodied in critical articles and reviews.

Life Magic books are available at MMH Press

www.mmhpress.com

Because of the dynamic nature of the Internet, any web addresses or links contained in this book may have changed since publication and may no longer be valid. The views expressed in this work are solely those of the authors and do not necessarily reflect the views of the publisher and the publisher hereby disclaims any responsibility for them.

The author (s) of this book do not dispense medical advice or prescribe the use of any technique as a form of treatment for physical, emotional, or medical problems without the advice of a physician, either directly or indirectly. The intent of the author(s) is only to offer information of a general nature to help you. In the event you use any of the information in this book for yourself, which is your constitutional right, the author(s) and the publisher assume no responsibility for your actions.

ISBN: (hc) 978-0-9945265-8-8

ISBN: (e) 978-0-9942850-6-5

Dedication

This book is dedicated to Donna.

Thank you for your unwavering belief and support,
and for always being wonderful you.
With love, Karen

Acknowledgements

This book would not be if it were not for my forever friend and quite often advisor, Donna. You seen something in me that I couldn't see in myself. You believed in me and in turned I began to believe in myself. Thank you from the bottom of my heart. I am eternally grateful for you.

To my family who I miss every day, thank you for not giving up on me when you quite easily could have. I love you all.

To my husband, thank you for my learning and for your love.

To my beautiful children, you are my everything, my world works because of you.

To all of my close friends who lift me every day, I am so grateful to have you in my life.

Thank you to Teena for proofing this book.

Thank you to the powers that be, you have blessed me with an amazing adventure, I promise to make the most of it.

Contents

Preface

Section 1: The Journey

Spiritual Journey 1
A New Life 4
Full Circle 11
Embracing the Dream 25

Section 2: Mindful musings

Spirituality 30
Consciously connecting with your inner spirit 35
Expectations 41
Simple things 44
A helping hand of kindness 46
Conscious minds 49
Go within or go without 54
Positive thinking 59
The Push 64
Are we responsible for the effect we have on others? 70
Forgiving spirit 74
Personal evolution: To become a butterfly? 78
Embracing the Butterfly 80
What do you choose for yourself today? 83
Awakening 87

Changing lanes..91
How time goes by 95
Reach for the stars...98
Our universal minds 101
Gratitude..106
Choices and values, past or present?..................111
Wisdom 114
Great Thinkers 114
Inspiration...118
I'm a believer..123
Why do we label?..127
How to stop labelling 129
A woman's touch 131
The moment..132
How we adjust 134
Friendship...138
Can you keep a secret?......................................143
Happiness 148
Our outer glow..152
The cycle of life 156

Section 3: Law of loving attraction

The Spiritual Law of Love 162
Loving Law of Attraction: The Mirror Effect 166
Loving Law of Attraction: A tortoise or a hare? 170

Loving Law of Attraction: Ask – Believe – Receive ... 173

Loving Law of Attraction: A negative path 177

Loving Law of Attraction: To catch a fish! 180

The answer is 'LOVE' 183

Section 4: Through the Darkness

Why it is important to embrace life's spiritual struggles 190

Healthy minds 194

When you feel your world is falling apart 197

Becoming more aware 200

Tough times revisited 201

Positively dealing with trauma 204

Drama therapy 211

Sharing your story is all part of the healing process 213

Section Five: Heart Writer

Healing the write way 216

Spirit writing 220

Do you dream of writing? 222

How did writing find you? 225

Writing 228

About Karen Weaver 247

Preface

There was a special time in my life when I wrote articles for a website called Building Beautiful Bonds. I wrote these articles throughout my period of enlightenment (2010 to 2012) and I believe there are a few hidden gems amongst this collection.

I remember the overwhelming buzz I felt every time inspiration touched me. I enthusiastically sat at my computer typing out almost one thousand words and then hitting send to the site administrator. The excitement I felt when they went live was special indeed. I proudly printed them off and added the newest addition to my file, which I still have. This file would only come out for my mum when she visited. She was so proud and this was, for me, the ultimate achievement.

Over the years many of these articles have been picked up for publication in *Universal Mind* magazine.

Imagine my elation whilst revisiting each one only to discover that many have been viewed more than two thousand times. This was affirmation enough for me to choose a number of them to put together in this book. I hope you enjoy reading them as much as I enjoyed writing them.

Spiritual Journey

If someone had mentioned a Spiritual Journey to me a few years ago I would have said, "What a load of mumbo jumbo." However after experiencing a life-changing transition I have never been more at peace with myself. I do not feel it is necessary to find God or any other godly figure to have a spiritual journey. I feel it is what happens within one's own soul that changes our outlook on ourselves and our place in life itself and all for the better.

I have found a peaceful happy place within, which I would not swap for all the money in the world. There can be no price put on it but if its essence could be bottled it would be a heavenly scent. The book *Eat, Pray, Love* by Elizabeth Gilbert describes one woman's spiritual journey to happiness within and it has been a best seller and made into a movie starring Julia Roberts.

This shows we can all feel inspired by other people's journeys of self-discovery. But what we need to remember is that it doesn't have to be a dramatic life altering and big family upheaval type of self-journey. We don't all need to dump our hubbies and go travelling. We might just need to take time out for ourselves without feeling guilty.

Find a balance that works for you, enjoy it, and embrace the changes in your perceptions of the things around you and yourself. Allow your values to alter and your dreams to change. Do not be afraid of the natural process this journey brings. You will be a more balanced individual because of it, never failing to learn more and loving each day that brings new things your way. If you are aware, you will learn something new every day.

I am lucky that I have truly found ME. I can sincerely say I am deeply happy and fulfilled as a person. Don't get me wrong, I am no saint. I still make mistakes and learn every day from them but I now have a more positive outlook and am more aware of others. I feel so privileged to have been given this opportunity to get to where I am even though it has been a rough journey.

Who would have known that the one person who was the cause of such upheaval in my life would actually end up being my saviour? I listened to my intuition, which was shouting loud within, 'Through conflict comes change'. I knew things couldn't go on the way they were. My life was not my own and I lived as a puppet for others.

I went with what my heart was telling me and it has worked out for me. It was a gamble but it has paid off. I had to learn something very hard for me as a pleasing Piscean —to say, 'Sorry, but NO' without the guilt of feeling I had let others down. I learned a lot by this alone and I have never looked back.

I am now an at-home mum and I could not be happier. I have come from being a hard-working go-getter trying to make something of myself so my family would be proud of me whilst also trying to please others constantly. The transition to being proud of me was a challenging one and many instilled values I was taught throughout my childhood have changed. They were not all bad but they didn't fit me so I traded them in for some snug-fitting values.

We will all eventually get to a crossroads at some point in our lives where we can make the choice to change if we are not happy with how things are going on our life journey, or we can choose to stay on the same road. No matter which road we choose, there will be challenges but if we are in touch with ourselves and in a more positive place, this will ultimately assist us in dealing with them. It can also mean we will be happier with less and embrace the things in life that mean the most to us. I hope everyone gets the opportunity to experience a spiritual journey of their own because life can mean so much more when we are comfortable in our own skin.

A New Life

I am about to board the plane. Heading Down Under. What should I be feeling? What do I feel? I don't know, maybe numbness if I had to pick something, everything seems so surreal. Maybe this is how my body and mind deal with dramas now. Get on with the task in hand and deal with the impact later. Or more likely I have gone into auto pilot. I am thirty-five weeks pregnant after all. The full impact of this dramatic life change could hit any time and I may not make it to Australia, but I must remember it is not just me to consider, there are my two young sons and my husband too.

We are starting a new life together as a complete family unit. This is what I really want for us, but why do I not feel really excited? Where are the butterflies that should be doing somersaults in my tummy with anticipation? Maybe what I am sacrificing to fulfil my dream is so much that it all balances itself out to a feeling of nothing. How sad that thought is. However, it is not going to change anything thinking like that. I have decided to change things in my life and my goodness, how I have changed things. I can only hope and pray it all turns out well and that I made the right decision two years ago in the depths of anxiety. Have I been stubborn and stupid or am I adventurous and wise?

The last few years have been torturous to my soul. The independent go-getter got a psychological battering and didn't feel safe in her own skin any longer. I will be honest and say that I felt totally betrayed by each and every one in my family when they reacted the way they did when my brother went crazy in my home. The effects of post-traumatic stress are shocking. It shakes from the core and it created a great darkness inside of me that caused me to close the shutters to the outside world. I started to live day by day trying to do the best for my partner and children. I left my job which I loved and my home felt different because flashbacks frequently occurred.

    I felt no reason to stay somewhere that made me and my family unhappy. There was no longer anything holding me back from our dream of moving to Australia so we applied for our visas. When I let everyone know our plans their disbelief was not unexpected. They thought I wouldn't actually see it through and that I was just running away from everything, But they also knew that once I have my mind set on something I never give up until I have succeeded - but then again, they thought that side of me was not around anymore.

    For a full year afterwards our luck was shocking. Not only was I trying to keep strong for my family but everything we did or touched went wrong. I remember the cars, how much bad luck we had with cars over that time. Even the car Dad lent me blew a radiator within a week. It couldn't just be maintenance issues, there had to be bad luck in it too. The engine seized in the sporty car that we bought and paid dearly to make the way we wanted. What are the chances of that? Mind you, if that had been all, I could have dealt with it as they were just material things.

    The time I thought our luck had changed was when I discovered I was pregnant. There seemed to be light gleaming from the end of the tunnel and oh, how I wanted it so much. I couldn't wait to tell everyone and then to discover that little sis was expecting too for the same time was fantastic. I finally felt happiness again and I was making plans in my head. The morning I discovered the blood was indescribable. "Why me?" was all I could think. I rested in bed in a desperate attempt to save the pregnancy but one week later it disappeared. I know exactly when it happened as I lay there analysing every movement in my uterus. I was distraught and my partner was such a rock for me in my vulnerable state, even though he was feeling the loss too. He had done so much over the last week to make things easier. I remember just lying at nights, feeling empty and praying to be full again. I knew the pain would not go away until I filled that void, the feeling was uncontrollable. If anything good was to come out of the whole experience it was that it made me feel protected and so loved by my strong partner and it brought us so close again. That was when we decided to get married. When I look back now, it was as if the diamond dazzler that he bought me changed my life. I know now that it was at that point our luck changed.

    We booked the wedding for May and in February we discovered I was expecting again. Everything was changing for the better. Of course, initially the fear of possibly loosing another pregnancy hit me but I took it easy. Then there was the wedding to organise in just a few months. It wasn't ideal to be slowing down, but so what, the main thing was that things seemed to be working out for a change. All of the rest would fall into place.

I remember the day I went to pick up our rings. It was the brightest, sunniest day of the year so far. I had a glow around me and a smile on my face again. No one or nothing was going to drag me down. I was at the counter paying for the rings when my phone rang. It was the visa application centre and the Australian migration department had granted our visas, we could now become full residents of Australia if we wanted. "Oh my goodness, what a year, what a turn of luck," is what I initially thought and also that I must remember to do the Lotto.

We had to enter Australia before December, our baby was due in October and we had no visa for her so we had no choice but to go soon. In one year to get married, finish building a house, migrate to the other side of the world and have a baby. These are things people do over their lifetime, not all in one year. It has to be done though, everything happens for a reason is what I kept telling myself and others. I am just going to enjoy these good times and not take anything for granted ever again.

The wedding was great, low key and we did what we wanted, which was sweet and intimate and enjoyed by all. The flowers were lilies and the man from the flower shop lent us tall vases for them. The scene of me and my sisters running into the chapel a few days after the wedding to retrieve the vases still sticks with me to this day. The chapel is close to my heart as it was where my mum and dad got married, my granny always attended and I felt her spirit with me there, my children were christened there and the priest was non-judgmental and fun. In fact he had a motor bike and hung out with all walks of life and he worked hard to get the young people back to mass

The finishing of the house was not all plain sailing. My new hubby was doing most of the work himself and time was quickly going on. We still had not got our tickets booked for Australia as money was tight and what we had we needed to finish the house. Everything was up in the air. It was now July and I did not know where I was going or what our plans were going to be for the next six months. I was getting bigger and bigger every day and my pregnancy was a bit tough but we stayed focused on getting things ready for leaving even though we had no flights booked.

Then we did it, we gathered the money to get our tickets and booked them for the first of September, the first day of spring in Australia and the first day of autumn in Ireland. Those next few weeks were surreal to say the least. So much to organise but 'where there is a will there is always a way'. It rained a lot during that time. I remember a lot of darkness in the weather and a lot of disbelief that I was actually going. I was running from pillar to post trying to spend time with my family, get ready for leaving and preparing finances. Over the years we had accumulated a lot of things which we put into the new garage and told our families to take what they liked. We got the new house completed just in time, which was a huge challenge in itself. I don't know how my hubby did it all himself, but he did. I wasn't much help waddling around.

Families from both sides organised some leaving parties, which was so nice of everyone. It is good to have those memories to take with us and nice to leave with positive thoughts, even if they were filled with a lot of emotion. However I do remember my sister saying that it was as if I was dying and preparations were being made accordingly, as pictures of me were being hung up all over the family home.

The morning came and it was time to go. The last week had been so exhausting mentally and physically as we prepared for our departure. We were so close to going nowhere as our finances had fallen through a few days earlier. We stuck with it and didn't give up and it has paid off. If it is worth having, it is worth fighting for and it makes you appreciate it all the more. I went up to my family home where everyone had gathered to say goodbye. All was very strange and I was again numb to emotion. There was the usual banter that happens when all of the family gathers, which was good as it kept everything going. My parents and sister had been to a wedding the night before and to my horror my father was still quite under the influence. This was a bit of a problem because he was to chauffeur us to the airport. It was strange, as my father was never a real drinker at all. However my brother-in-law came to the rescue and offered to drive us. We said our last goodbyes and I tried my best to hold back the tears. With a big lump in my throat we drove away. I dropped my son off at his father's house to say goodbye to his grandparents and other relations and his dad was following us to the airport so that he could see him off.

The journey to the airport was not an easy one. We were squashed in the back of a car, my two-year-old was impatient, my tipsy father was in the passenger seat not feeling very well and he did not smell very well either come to think of it, which did not help me in my situation. Then there were all of the detours because of road works and we got lost. It wasn't really going to plan but we had left in good time. When we finally got to the airport I said a quick goodbye and fled as I felt tears coming. Inside the terminal there was another problem. Where was my eldest son? I had thoughts of his father abducting him and all sorts of things. But by the skin of his teeth he arrived so we went and checked in at the desk.

As we getting ready to enter the terminal my phone rang. It was my in-laws who had come to surprise us at the airport. "Oh no more tears" is what I thought initially as I knew I was on the verge of letting all of mine flow out. We said more goodbyes and got through to the gate where, phew, we could now breathe. To say I was on an emotional rollercoaster would be an understatement and I still had numerous hours of flying and no sleeping to face. I do hope it has all been worth it. It is now time for us to depart from our previous life to set up another on the other side of the world. My journey to departures has now ended and a new chapter of my life has begun.

Full Circle

There was a period in my life, not so long ago, when I had become a slave to expectation. Not any expectation that was imposed upon me but an expectation that I had imposed onto myself to meet the needs of others, and I was sacrificing too much of myself in the process. I felt like I was living my life for everyone else and not myself. I was playing follow the leader, whereas I was used to being my own leader. I did not realise that it didn't have to be this way. To allow myself something would not result in me losing it all; in fact in hindsight, it would enhance my experience of life, and because I was happier those around me would reap the benefits also. I needed to find the 'me' that I had lost a time back. I needed to keep moving forward and get back to the happy vibrant glowing me that I once was. I needed to turn full circle.

My Childhood

I was the first born into my family. I was prayed for because my parents had lost their first pregnancy, and as they were not long married when this happened, they felt the loss terribly. My father glows when he recounts to me how I was the spitting image of him when I was born. My mother laughs that I was a full month overdue; she was lying in the hospital for weeks, and every attempt to induce labour was not successful. When I finally decided to make an appearance into the world, I had outgrown some of my skin, namely on my bottom, and my parents were not allowed to take me home with them when it was time to leave the hospital a week later. Things were done a lot slower those days in Ireland. Mum has often recalled to me the excitement of getting up one morning and dashing to the phone box to phone the hospital and see how I was when she was given the news that the doctor had cleared me to go home. As we had no family car, mum recalls that she ran down to the main road and hitch-hiked a lift to the big town and ordered a taxi to take me and her home. When my father arrived home on his lunch break from the local factory, mum had me propped up on the sofa and never said a word until he saw me sitting there like a 'mini me'. Now family life could begin.

I have always felt lucky to have been given the parents that I have. I have always had a close connection with my dad; it is an unspoken natural bond that I treasure dearly, and looking back it has always given me a secure foundation on which to grow. But it is my mum who raised us all; she has always encouraged me to live my dreams and been a support through the good times and the bad. She is one of those mums that you can call on anytime, no judgements and no expectations.

My parents came from different situations; they were raised on the same street yet experienced life so differently. My father was cared for by his grandparents when he was young. My mother was number six in a household of twelve children. When my mum and dad got together and started a family, it is understandable that they wanted to create a loving home and a secure loving family bond so that their children could flourish out into the world with the stability and support of loving parents.

Looking back on my young childhood, I know that I was very fortunate to have been given my parents and I never take that for granted. I have and still do learn so much from them. Christmases and Birthdays have always been very special and my mum always makes a lot of effort no matter what else is going on at the time. I believe in the magic of life because of my mum's efforts.

I always felt very much loved; this feeling of unconditional love has stayed with me and made me feel safe and indestructible. I was the first born of six, three girls and then three boys. Family was always everything to me; we all have always had a very strong bond, and I have always felt a huge loyalty to my family. I never imagined living one day of my life without contact let alone living the other side of the globe with the prospect of never seeing them again; however, life sometimes has a strange way of directing us in alternative directions than what we expect, and I have learned to not resist unexpected changes, as they often have a positive outcome.

A big change for me, when I was young, was when we moved from the Republic of Ireland to the North of Ireland. Even though we only geographically shifted one and a half miles 'out the road', it was a major change in lifestyle and thinking. We were leaving the close-knit community of town life to embrace a more isolated existence in the countryside. It is all part of my journey to where I am now and my parents were fulfilling a dream to build a house on a hill and I always remember feeling so proud of that.

Looking back on my childhood, now that I am a mum myself, I know that we all are still learning about life even when we become parents and that as children we just expect our parents to be perfectly grounded when in actual fact they are still human and can make mistakes also. I consider myself fortunate because my parents did, and still do, everything with the right intention and for our family and through them I have learned so much about life. When you have that kind of support you never feel alone.

When I was sixteen I chose not to stay at school and I applied for a job in a factory, which I got. It felt good to earn my own money. I then moved back to a job in my home town. It felt perfect, something shifted in me when that happened; it was as if I had come home as if I belonged again. I felt more grounded and had a desire to set some foundations to my life. I was more settled and started going out with someone who I had known since my early school years. I felt grown up; I began wanting things like a home, a commitment, and a baby, and that is how it happened.

When, at eighteen, I discovered that I was pregnant it was quite a shock. My father was disappointed, which was to be expected, but my mother, she was such a great support and assured me that everything would be ok, a real rock when I needed it most. I know that without that support my pregnancy would have been a more negative experience.

Over the next year I grew up very quickly. I loved being a mum so much, my son was my life. I worked hard and was focused on moving forward, but unfortunately my partner did not grow up at the same speed I did and we drifted apart.

I was now a 20-year-old single mum, but with the support of my wonderful mum, I was able to keep working and moving forward. I had a blip where I had a distracting relationship with my supervisor who was ten years my senior, but that didn't evolve as I had hoped and we went our separate ways; he went to America, I stayed in the factory and was offered his supervisory position. Financially things were improving, and I was enjoying the unexpected new-found responsibility in my work. I decided to give it another go with my son's dad. I really made an effort, but I was soon to discover that we were still not compatible; however, I felt guilty and so stayed in the relationship longer than I should of. I was still only a young 23 at this stage. I finally found the courage to move forward and so I ended the relationship, and he moved to America (this was becoming a trend).

I changed my approach to life after that, and things became more positive for me again. I was enjoying being a single mum, and I had good friends around me and a wonderful relationship with my sister also. I left my supervisory job, and I found a part time job and went back to college. Money was tight, but money wasn't everything.

I was astounded to learn that I loved learning; I had never felt this way about knowledge before. It was as if I had caught a learning bug, and I needed to absorb all of the information I could find. I did a Foundation course and discovered that I loved English and media. The course was two years long and was not easy, but I juggled everything so well. I had balance, and my heart was singing.

When I was 25 I met someone; I didn't feel as though there was any room in my life for a relationship, but I decided after a while to give it a go with this person as he seemed keen and, although he was not my usual type as he had a bad-boy image, I connected with something in him. I realise now that it was his intention.

It was as if something shifted to allow this relationship to happen as my son's dad was back from America and he was keen to see him at the weekends. As my new partner worked away during the week, weekends were the only time we could get time together, and so I gave it a go. It soon became serious, and within six months I had moved out of my lovely little house and began setting up home with him and my son. I was to work harder to keep this all together. I had two jobs, I was finishing my course, and, as I did not want to change my son from his school, I ensured that I did all that I could to keep him there.

Then I met a crossroads. I was accepted into university but that meant shifting my whole life to the top of Ireland, and it didn't feel like the right time to do that. At the same time, an opening came up in administration that I was really interested in doing. I chose the job and to study humanities part time and I was offered another part-time job with the local college tutoring in out-centres. Everything I was asking for from life was happening, but I was juggling so much—college, two jobs, parenthood, a new relationship and commuting long distances. Something had to give, and when I lost my driving license for a year because of drunk driving, I was soon to realise that it was the commuting that was going to go. It was a tough year, but I managed to keep my jobs, complete my course, be there for my son and have a relationship. Lesson learned!

I was then offered a scholarship to a year-long, once-a-month intensive drama course; I had the opportunity to visit various locations all around Ireland, the only problem being that it was at weekends. Was I going to stretch things too far again? I chose to accept the scholarship, and although it was tough, I adjusted for that year. I discovered so many things about myself during the course as many of the things we explored directly connected with my inner self, this was something I would often shy away from facing. I didn't know if the outer me was really expressing what the inner me felt. My confidence was an issue on top of the list in addition to some incidents of intimidation throughout my life that had affected me deeply—one from my English teacher and one from a work mate who used to pick on me to make me blush really badly. It was intense, but it had to be, as we were being taught to go out there and help others overcome their social and personal problems through drama therapy. At the end of the course, we put on a production. I was astonished to discover that I could remember a script; I have never had the best memory. I loved this experience! Because of the qualification I got from the course I was offered a position through the local college teaching drama to adults with special needs. I loved this job so much and found it was very natural for me to give in this way to others. It was hard work but so rewarding.

The play we staged at the end of my course 'Lipstick Powder and Politics' was chosen to tour, I was so excited, but what I didn't know is that I was actually pregnant at the time and so I had to pull out. That was ok though because my partner and I were so excited and had been trying for a baby for some time and it hadn't been happening and with my new job I knew that it was a sign to focus on what I had already achieved.

We had recently bought a block of land with an old house on it, and we decided to do it up and make it liveable until we built a new house on the block.

The U-turn

There was something about that house. I loved the quaintness of it, but things began going downhill when we moved there. It was as if life had done a u-turn and was steadily going downhill. The only good thing that happened over the next two years was the healthy birth of our son. I felt like I was being made pay for anything I did wrong in my life. It was a tough time, and after an incident occurred that sunk me low enough to suffer post-traumatic stress, we decided to embark on setting up a whole new life for ourselves in Australia. Luckily, I knew what was wrong with me, as I had been working in a Mental Health setting for a number of years, and I allowed myself to be guided through my recovery by listening to my inner spirit. I slowed my life way down, and for the next year I took each moment as it came and dealt with life accordingly. I was getting stronger each day.

We began building the new house and, in the back of our minds, hoped to get a residency visa to Australia, but if we didn't then at least we would have a new family home. I was just going along with things during this time, and when I discovered I was expecting, it was light—a positive light—shining into our lives again. I had not considered having another child but it seemed so right and I felt a glow again. This was to be a short-lived elation as I was to miscarry a few weeks later. I was distraught, I couldn't stop crying. I wanted that baby so much; it was going to make everything better again. I prayed so hard every single night that I would be filled again as I felt so empty. I couldn't understand why this happened to me. It was during this time my partner, who was my rock, and I also received great support from my parents which brought us all closer again. But what I didn't realise then is that this harrowing time in my life was to shift me back onto my right path. It was the wakeup call that I had needed. Everything started to fall into place. My relationship was back on track, and my partner proposed. This was in December, and we booked the wedding for May. It felt so right. I saw how strong my partner was when I really needed him, and it made me feel so protected, which I really needed at the time.

Choosing to get married was a really big deal for me as I had always said that I was never going to get married and contentment was my worst enemy, but now I had changed my thinking on this and the actions were following. Contentment was what I craved and getting married felt like the next step for me.

Then it all came together

It was as if the angel of all good things came knocking on our door. I discovered that my prayers had been answered and I was expecting again. We then received notification that we had been granted full residency status for Australia. This was going to be a busy year! What a transition. It was as if we had jumped off the treadmill of life that made me feel as if I was going nowhere, just getting slower and slower; however, I now realise that this was my preparation time, and my wait was now over. I was now ready to run the gauntlet of life again.

Moving to Australia was something I know that I was destined to do. I was thirty-one when we moved. It has given me the space that I so desperately needed to grow within myself. I now know what people mean when they say that they 'found themselves'; I truly did. I don't know if I needed to move to the other side of the world to do this but I did need space in which to deal with all of the raw emotions that come with evolving this way.

A few weeks after we arrived in Australia, I had my third child, and my creativity blossomed. I was so connected to parenthood, and I began writing and illustrating children's books. I was making myself happy and my children happy. In one year, I wrote and illustrated about thirty books for my children.

I then fell pregnant again for my fourth child. I know that being pregnant has allowed me to be emotional. I have given myself permission to be vulnerable; many see this as a weakness, I now class it as strength.

I went through a rough patch were, through my thoughts and dreams, I relived situations of my past. Even years later, these situations needed me to feel the suppressed emotions that I had hidden deep down inside me. I have embraced forgiveness—forgiveness of myself as well as others—and this has freed me from the shackles of the past to allow me to move forward.

I realised then that life is learning and everything that we encounter in our lifetime is in the best interest in the advancement of our spirit and it is individual to us. Whether someone is a positive or a negative influence in my life, I still learn from them. Whether it is momentary or for a time, I have learned something from each interaction I have had, and it is important to deal with the emotions that surface because that helps us to grow as a person.

This cleansed me, my heart opened up, and I was ready to embrace life again. I had allowed myself to connect with my inner guide, and all of a sudden I understood things. I was thinking for myself again, whereas I hadn't wanted that responsibility for some time because of the consequences that may arise from my choices. Fear was limiting me from embracing life fully. I chose to honour the fear that I felt and to follow my heart by replacing it with love.

Discovering my inner writer!

My beautiful friend, Donna, introduced me to her new website, and it was called Adopt a Mum. I decided to join, and here I was introduced to new and exciting things. I began writing in the groups and got such wonderful responses that I began writing longer pieces. It wasn't long before I was writing weekly articles about things I was discovering about my spiritual journey. Writing was giving me a way to release so much from inside. I couldn't stop. I was receiving signs from all around, and the serendipity of the signs that were happening amazed me. I realised that I had become more aware of life on a different level. I was living on a different frequency and attracting things more easily because of that.

It was when my fourth child was four weeks old that I embarked on the mission to write a book. At first I did not have a clue what I was going to write about; I had never planned or written a story before, so I wasn't 100% sure what I needed to do. All I knew is that it felt so right and everything was aligned for me to achieve it. The chain of serendipitous events happened like this: I was first introduced to the possibility of writing 50000 words by my beautiful friend when she told me that she had sat down and written 50000 words about her life. This flipped the switch of possibility on, and I was so inspired by this possibility. Then, in my inbox came a message from an annual challenge which invited writers to write 50000 words in a month by meeting a daily target of 1667 words. Again, I just knew that it was right for me. But what was I going to write about?

I then had a surreal experience when one day I was watching *'The View'* and there was a celebrity couple on who had suffered a miscarriage; I felt their pain. Whoopi Goldberg stopped the show to say to them that she tells her girlfriends that when someone miscarries it is a Visitor that has come to prepare them for receiving the true gift because maybe they weren't on the right path or ready. This resonated with me beyond belief, I was uplifted, and in that instant I had been gifted with the spiritual understanding of why I had experienced a miscarriage. I felt compelled to share this with others to help them. Within a few days I began the writing challenge, and one month later *The Visitor ~ a magical understanding of uncertainty* was finished.

I know that my writing may conjure up unwanted feelings in some people; however, I do write with the truest of intention, which is to help others heal and see an alternative perspective—some people are ready and some people are not, and that is fine.

I put it out there into the universe that I really wanted to have this book published and it was. The gorgeous person who introduced me to the possibility of actually writing a book was also the person who made the opportunity available for me to publish my book. This lady has definitely had a profoundly positive impact on my life as a friend and someone who believes in me so much. I will always be truly grateful to her for being such a positive in my life.

As my book was being published I learned so much about the whole process of book publishing. So when the opportunity found me early 2012 to set up *Inner Light Publishing*, I listened to my heart and I knew it was the right thing to do. Since then it has grown at a steady and magical pace. Everything we needed to know came to us just as we needed to know it. Our vision is clear: we want to share as many stories with others as we can and this we will do. It also turned out that we are helping authors and community groups self-publish their books economically and positively. When we follow our hearts, things come together effortlessly.

I have had my work published on adoptamum.com, in publications all over the world as well as in a monthly magazine called *Universal Mind*, and I have even had the opportunity to be published on mamamia.com. I have since written and published the next book in *The Enlightenment Series* called *The Wish Giver*, and I am soon to finish *The Memory Taker*.

The lessons I have learned so far is that spiritually we are on this earth to grow. We all work towards the same goal of enlightenment within, some of us acknowledge it and have an easier ride and others don't. I have learned to forgive everyone and everything; this is for my greater good. I endeavour to ensure that everything I do is executed with the truest of intention. I have also realised that I cannot be responsible for how others react to me but I can be responsible for how I react to others.

I have embraced the universal *Law of Attraction* in a spiritual way, and I know that by releasing positive, loving energy out into the world I am doing my bit to attract it back to me. I choose not to feel fear; I choose to live in the power that I have been gifted with, and I choose to live my best life. To further enhance my knowledge on the power of attraction, I have completed Advanced Law of Attraction training, and I am now a certified practitioner.

I have now rotated full circle and live my life, once again, with passion and love, and this makes my heart sing!

I truly do live *MY* dream! Being a mum to five wonderful children and being able to write and help others is what I am destined to do, it feels so right and I am grateful to have the opportunity to feel so fulfilled, there are many people who never find what it is that makes their heart sing and I have so much that makes mine beat a harmonious tune every day.

I know that I may have challenges to face in my lifetime, but now I can face them with a renewed understanding of life. I have been fortunate to come to this understanding at a young age, and it will help me give the best of myself to others and that is what I endeavour to do. I am living the perfect life for me. I have created it for myself, and I am grateful for it every day. I encourage everyone to keep a little for yourself—do something that makes your heart sing!

I have come *Full Circle* as I now live my life with passion and love again. My secret recipe to being happy is to embark on life with the right intention, be willing to adjust your perspective when need be, be aware of the bigger picture of what is going on around you, and listen to your inner guide; you will know when things are right for you and waste less time steering off your true path. Finally, love yourself; you are your own best friend.

I do hope that you have enjoyed reading my journey thus far; I know that I have still so much to experience from life but this I do with a greater sense of awareness and an overwhelming appreciation to my family and loved ones who show me so much support even when I falter.

I have added a piece I wrote about my journey, physically and emotionally, to Australia, I hope that from my journey you may gain some insight.

Embracing the Dream

I have always been a person who followed my heart. This has often gotten me into bother and even though I have always had the most sincere intentions of not knocking anyone over on my way towards achieving my dreams I have on occasion bumped into people on my journey.

I look back on my 37 years thus far and WOW is all that I can say. I have been very blessed in many ways. I did go through a dark period in my early 30's but I was fortunate enough to have been enlightened as a consequence of it and so I am grateful for the insights into my depths that I have received because I am now a more complete and wholesome person for experiencing them. I will not go into detail about my journey to enlightenment as I wrote about that in detail in *Journey to Inner Light* that has already been published and some readers of *Living a Positive Life* may have already read it.

Wisdom is something that I have come to value immensely. Simplicity is underrated in my view and we as human beings make life way more complicated than it needs to be. I have discovered that our first reaction to things is often an emotional one and that the head comes in to create balance at a later stage and it is then that we should react. I watched an interview that Oprah had with an Irish Author who wrote a book filled with this type of observations. It made sense when he said that with a confrontation it takes more to step back and let it pass by. Detach yourself from the situation immediately. This can often be perceived by the naive as an act of cowardly behaviour but in my experience it takes more courage to take that step back and any regrets that I have in my life come from not taking that step back as the consequence of the alternative can send ripples throughout someone's life, altering it without even thinking!

I suppose having children has focused my attention elsewhere. I am now a mum to 5 children and I don't want them making the mistakes that I made but I decided early on not to dwell on that. I choose to parent with love and it has served me well so far. Don't get me wrong; I am no angel and I have yelped a few times but my focus is to parent through love and when my children have something that they need to learn I guide them firmly with love through that issue. I don't like instilling fear into them as I feel that doing that harms their emotional wellbeing and only shows them how to instill fear in others and let's be honest, the world does not need many more people with that mentality.

I have embraced wholeheartedly the principle of the Law of Attraction and although there are many things that affect my life that I don't control I know that I can control how I react to them and I am always conscious about thinking about everything as positively as I can. Making the best out of every given situation is something I have inherited from my mum; she is a very resilient woman who always does her best to pursue a positive outcome even in the most negative of situations.

That is why her latest challenge is her biggest test of all. I am living at the other side of the world and sometimes feel useless in her dealing with her challenge. I know that by remaining positive and being that someone she can ring anytime, I am doing a little bit. I am also only a plane ride away and I am very grateful that the world is not as hugely limiting as it once was.

As conscious as I am of the miraculous things that are possible through fully focusing on what vibrations you are sending out, there it is tremendously hard to control the feelings connected to someone you love being sick. This is when I allow myself to honour them, have a huge cry and call in my friends for support; then when the surge of emotion pass I find that I am more clear of mind to make decisions. In the past I would have bottled it up but that is not helping anyone. By releasing and taking positive action I am instigating the best possible outcome.

I am very lucky that I live a positive life, I am grateful for it and because of this I know that I will continue to live a positive life because life is often about perspective. If you believe in the positive then positive will find you.

I am able to stay at home with my children and that is a really wonderful thing for me. Because of this I have been able to write books and pursue an interest in publishing books also. I now own Serenity Press Publishing and even though we are a small publishing press now I know that it can be as big or small as I want it to become. I am amazed at how far we have progressed in such a short period of time that is totally by believing that anything is possible, not setting limitations and embracing opportunities as they arise. I am able to help authors bring their dream of becoming a published author to life in a positive way and that is a wonderful thing.

On a more personal note, my third novel is about to go to print. I have seven journals published and I have also created Mamma Macs Home-made Children's books. These are books that I created with and for my children which we have decided to publish and in doing so we are raising money for a children's charity because they were created through love and wonderful things need to come out of their publication. I will write more about writing and my journey in our next collection *Writing the Dream.*

I try my best to be true to myself while still being the type of mum, wife, daughter, sister and friend that I can be given my circumstances. We all have choices and our choices determine our life. I have created the life that I have by doing what I feel is best in every situation and following my heart when I can. I don't embrace everything as the timing is not right when some things present themselves but I always like to remember a quote that always sticks with me, "What is for you will never pass you." If you want to experience something and the timing is not right, it will come back to you at a later stage.

I think that the best advice I can share with anyone is to be true to you. If you really want something, pursue it; those who love you will support you if you want it enough, and be patient because then you will enjoy the process of achieving your dreams as it is important to savour our beautiful lives.

Mindful Musings

Spirituality

I have come across many definitions of 'spirituality' but the one I connected with is:

"The meaning of spirituality is diving deep into the inner self and realizing our true identity. The spirit within! It is only through the path of spirituality that human beings have gained enlightenment."

I think that being or becoming spiritual is to progress within ourselves. To be able to love ourselves and others unconditionally and also to forgive more easily. It is a personal process which we may or may not choose to embark on in our lifetime, but it is widely recognised that those who do embark on their spiritual journey arrive at a point of personal fulfilment like no other. Connecting with our soul and helping it flourish to its highest potential is the most beautiful experience of all for many.

When talking about spirituality I am not talking about going to a regular service because you think it is the right thing to do or because you feel you have to. I mean going within and then going to a service from that point if that is what you feel meets with your personal spiritual requirements and beliefs.

In this era there is so much horror and devastation on global and personal levels for many. Belief that there is a higher source with our best intentions as its main focus, ensuring we are protected and that our needs and desires are being taken care of, is quite a comforting thought, especially through times of uncertainty.

If every human being recognised the power of the love and forgiveness principle, all consciousness on Earth would change instantly" Kuan Yin.

Forgiveness

The ability to forgive ourselves and others is a gift. This gift must not be abused or taken advantage of. This ability allows us to learn and move on in progression through our journey of life. When I speak of forgiveness for ourselves I don't mean someone who does not want to learn from their wrong-doing. These people are just being reckless but maybe at some point on their journey through life they may awaken to experience the beauty of looking at the world from within.

Giving.

The ability to give to others is not only a gift to them but a gift to ourselves because we are also giving ourselves the wonderful feeling of giving. And by doing so we are creating more opportunities for others to give and experience the same feeling. In order to have the honour of giving we must also be open to receiving. This cycle is a soul-enhancing experience. By using the word *giving* I am expressing giving our time, energy and love; however for some the giving of a material gift is used to represent their affections. "It is the thought that counts."

Five stages of the soul

It is usually when we start to query our being that we ask ourselves questions. The book *The five stages of the soul* by H.R Moody is an interesting book. It expresses how each of us transcends through different stages when we connect within. "Is this all there is?" is often a trigger question which instigates an urge to explore our spirituality because fulfilment in material and ambitious driven targets do not feed the soul.

1.   The Call: First step in the pursuit of spiritual wisdom. In history some have recorded dramatic callings, such as the roar from an ocean or other physical callings, but for most of us the CALL comes in less dramatic ways. Something just clicks or something occurs that draws us internally to start our journey. This can happen at any age or stage of our life cycle.

2.   The Search: Our response to 'The Call' is with a 'Search'. This happens for most as a search for guidance. A search for a spiritual teaching path or a seeking after a place within us where our spiritual impulse lives and grows. "We must try to rediscover the Friend in our hearts every moment. Our search is to keep remembering what we already know."

3.   The Struggle: Our guidance is discovered and our soul's true passage begins. This occurs in a cosmic dimension as well as a human one. Enduring challenges, trials or passing tests all may present themselves during this stage. These challenges can range from depression to debt to work issues to relationship issues to name a few. To reach the goal we must face the challenges head on.

4.   The Breakthrough: And then there was peace! Just like a miracle we will catapult to a state of at-oneness with something beyond ourselves. A sudden surge of energy pushes things to the limit; then follows a

burst of vision and the hidden forces of the world force to our consciousness. Something has changed in us, and we are never the same. Now known by some as 'The Changed Ones'.

5. The Return: Life goes on as before, but we now have a knowledgeable insight and understanding to give back to the world. Some may be a better more giving individual, others may become deeply committed to services or humanitarian projects. Those who experience a deeper experience of 'The Breakthrough' will likely develop as a guide or mentor.

Spiritual Practices

Meditation, Prayer and Contemplation are all used as techniques to develop our inner growth. It is believed that these practices lead to experiencing a feeling of connectedness to a larger reality. This can lead to a deeper sense of fulfilment within us and with others, nature and the universe. This can enable a person to discover the essence of their being; or the "deepest values and meanings by which people live".

Others may look outside of themselves to project blame onto a higher source. I would like to challenge that and ask that we go within and take on board our little piece of responsibility of how the world is changing. Maybe if we all were that little more loving and forgiving there would be less uncertainty.

For me, spirituality is getting to the point within myself where I can love myself and others unconditionally. No matter what happens, the ability to forgive and project love to even those who do us wrong is true divine peace within oneself.

I expect that as I progress on my eternal path to enlightenment my knowledge of spirituality will also progress. However, this is how I have come to understand a concept that is often thought of as complex, but if you take the time to listen to your inner guide you will soon discover it is all quite simple.

"The gifts we can receive from people who have tasted spiritual possibility are maps which we then use to guide our own journey." Ram Dass

Consciously connecting with your inner spirit

There are many wonderful people doing wonderful work connecting with spirits all the time. I applaud them and the energy they are surrendering in order to connect with their fabulous gift. I was lucky enough to connect with some wonderful men and women in this field when I was a guest speaker at the Psychic Development Association in Perth.

I was invited to talk about spirit writing. The type of spirit writing I am referring to is when we connect with our own spirit and share the wisdom and healing that is possible through this magnificent connection. So in light of this I would like to focus on the gift of connecting with our own spirit. Even though it is important for us to connect with the spirit of others, on both a physical and an afterlife level, it is my belief that connecting with our own spirit is of utmost importance.

When we allow ourselves the privilege of connecting with our own spirit we are opening up a new inner realm for ourselves, one that will fill us full of love, understanding, peace, wisdom and enlightenment. These are all the ingredients required to be at peace with ourselves and the world around us. Unless you have connected with your inner treasures you will not know what I am expressing. But trust me, when you seek refuge within, you will always be rewarded more generously than if you turn to an exterior source to ease the pain or fill a void.

Many of us are directed towards a life of education in order to get a good job – one that will help us sustain our physical needs and desires. We are also steered towards getting married and having a family, which also needs to be financially and emotionally sustained throughout our lifetime. In this fast-paced world we inhabit there seems not much time for reflection and connecting with ourselves. But should we take a little time to invest in our inner connection, we can experience working and family life at a far more fulfilling level.

Many of us choose to do good for others, maybe with thoughts of creating balance and positive karma for ourselves, or maybe because it makes us feel good to give back to the universe. We may do this by donating to those less fortunate or helping another in a time of need. It is wonderful for all involved when we are caring and giving but in order to advance in spirituality we need to listen to and cater to our own needs.

In times of hardship, self doubt and when searching for answers or reasons, we often turn to outside sources. Many of us seek solace in material possessions, or in an addiction of some sort or alternatively on a more supportive level, through a counsellor we go to as a last resort when things have become unbearable. But what is it those counsellors do? They try to guide us within by asking questions that may resonate and help us connect with why it has come to this. What does this tell us? Our answers are always within, waiting to be discovered. When we learn to connect, we can easily find the answer that is true to us and we can learn to deal with things before they become unbearable.

Wisdom and understanding will be provided to us when we need it the most, when we ask for it, when we listen to our inner self. This is a gift we have all been born with but as we grow up many of us disconnect with it. It is worth remembering that just because we get distracted and disconnect, that doesn't mean it is gone forever; it is always there waiting to be discovered.

How can we connect within?

Did you know that everyone is in touch with their inner spirit every day? But not everyone makes the mental connection. Have you ever been amazed at how a solution to a concern or problem comes to your mind? This is your spirit providing you with the wisdom you need to know at that moment.

Our spirit is precise and effective. We are not bombarded with wisdom we do not need; what we need to know will be revealed to us when we need it or when we ask. That is why people who consciously connect with their spirit live in peace and a magical knowing.

Many ways can be used to help us make the initial conscious connection with our inner spirit. My initial conscious connection was through a meditation and I now follow my connection through writing, but you can also use physical activities, prayer, writing or whatever works for you. I connected with my heart chakra; it was not just a spiritual connection, it was an actual physical connection where my heart fluttered quite definitely. I thought there was something physically wrong with me and visited specialists in search of the answer but they found me to be in perfect health, I did not consciously connect with the possibility that it was my loving spirit all along.

Here is a method you could use to consciously connect with your spirit:

Try to be in a quiet place with no distractions nearby and ensure that all potential disruptive noises are switched off or in silent mode. Position yourself in your most comfortable position ~ lying back, fully supported with your arms and legs relaxed. Take some deep slow breaths. Then allow yourself to breathe naturally and let your mind rest, let it be free from outside thoughts by pushing invasive thoughts away. When you feel you are in a deep peaceful place, ask your spirit a question.

Be patient and await a response. If you do not receive a response through your thoughts the first few times, do not be disheartened. You have not failed; your reply to your question will be revealed during an interaction with another or an encounter of some kind soon after. This is how spirit replies on many occasions. Keep yourself aware and open to receiving your response. The more you connect, the more natural it will become and often you will interact with your spirit without realising it.

It is important to remember that our spirit has our best interest at heart and will never steer us in the wrong direction. We must learn to trust and believe in our own abilities.

When we are in danger our spirit will let us know. We will feel unsettled, we will have an unexplained knowing that something is not how it should be. How many times have you thought to yourself '*I wish I had listened to myself!*'

Our spirit also connects with others. Have you ever thought about someone and then they contacted you? No matter the distance from someone, our spirits can transcend energy. If we really focus on another we may even feel what they are feeling. This is quite significant when we live parallel with other spirits. For example we can tap into how our partner, children or family/friends are feeling and will probably pick up on the frequency of their energy. That is why when someone we know and love is in pain we can sense it and have the ability to send them healing thoughts so that their spirit gains the benefit.

When we open ourselves to such possibilities it can be likened to an awakening as our senses are heightened. The physical vibration we omit when we transition is on a higher frequency and will be picked up on by others. You will more than likely discover that more positive people will come into your life. With that comes new opportunities. Our inner connection is a gift to be treasured and we can experience life on a different level because of this connection with ourselves. Our connection to our own spirit is our strength, security and encouragement through life. Why would you not take the chance? You have nothing to lose but so much to gain.

Expectations

Definition of expectation: *"A belief that something should happen in a particular way, or that something should have particular qualities or behavior."* – Macmillan Dictionary.

I have always had a thing about expectations. I believe they can be a root cause to a lot of negatives in our world today.

I once read that *"Expectations are the route of all anger"*. Take a moment to think about this. In a personal scenario when anger has been prominent, is it because one or other of the parties has had unfulfilled expectations? I have compared this to many situations in my life when I have experienced anger and I can say that *"Yes,"* on many of these occasions it has been because someone has had expectations of me in one way or the other.

I know that any time I have felt frustrated, it was because someone had not met my expectations. When I eliminated expectations I found I was more at peace with myself and others. Is the key to unlock the door of peace in this world losing our expectations?

A more universal example of an expectation could be if someone is not happy with the level of service they have received at a shop or other outlet. Should the level of service they expect not be met, they may get frustrated or even angry depending on how each individual reacts to their expectations being challenged. Have we a right to be angry in a case of this type? Probably yes, because someone is offering a service for a price and therefore selling you something. We have a right to expect to receive the service they are offering.

By not having expectations we will always be pleasantly surprised when something wonderful and unexpected comes our way.

Preventative expectations

We all expect. It is human nature. It can be a good thing in some ways as we may foresee potentially unpleasant occurrences and therefore prevent them. For example, if we see a banana skin on the floor and a guy walking right towards it, we would expect him to slip. Right? By intervening in time this may not happen. However it was expected to happen initially and that expectation resulted in action being taken to prevent that.

Emotional expectations

Some expectations can be emotionally damaging. The first thing that comes to mind for me is the high expectations some parents have of their children, adding extra pressure to their already stressful journey of discovery. Children strive naturally with our support, we don't need to push so much. They will find the right way on their own.

Expecting expectations

Why do we call it 'expecting' when we are pregnant? Already, before our beautiful little bundles of joy are even born we are expecting them! It seems that expectations are truly a part of our lives.

Self expectations

Possibly the person we expect the most of is ourselves. I know I push myself a little too much at times and try to make up for it later. Sometimes we can expect ourselves to do things that we would never in a million years expect anyone else to do. Can anyone relate?

Relationship expectations

This is when expectations can get emotionally intense, especially when things progress. Do you remember being a teenager waiting for your boyfriend or girlfriend to call? Even if they were one minute late you would be at your wits' end and if they got distracted, well that could be the worst thing ever. The teens of today are in constant contact with each other. How do they meet these expectations of constant contact?

I am sure there are many more areas of life when expectations are prominent. If we didn't have expectations we would rarely be disappointed, would we?

The best thing to keep in mind when expecting things from others is that most of the time anything others do for you is of their own free will and therefore a gift from them to you. If you expect it, then you take the gift away and turn it into a task. I know which I would rather have.

Let us keep our expectations low and our openness high.

Simple things

It is the simple things in life that our kids enjoy the most. Those simple things don't cost much, just the ability of adults to allow ourselves to see and maximise the opportunities. Kids will always find an opportunity to learn and have fun, we just need to direct them as best we can. A bee hopping from flower to flower, a butterfly fluttering around the garden or a leaf falling from a tree. How simple and natural are these examples?

In this day and age it can be so simple to forget that we as adults may know all about these things and take our knowledge foundations for granted but our kids don't know yet. Why let someone else have the joy of providing our kids with these facts when we can keep them ahead of the game by providing their growing minds with food for thought? Tell them about the bees' busy working life or the caterpillar's extraordinary journey to becoming a beautiful butterfly. These are amazing facts that kids will absorb and carry with them all of their lives and they will eventually share with their children.

My twenty-two-month old was looking out of the back door and said, "Mommy, a birdie". I knelt down beside her and we watched for a moment. A bird was busy building a nest in the tree. It flew into the tree with some twigs in its beak then back down to the ground to collect some more bits for its nest. Again and again this happened and my daughter was fascinated. Then I called my four-year-old to join us and they watched and absorbed the situation for a long time. Then my four-year-old had an idea to build his own nest so off to get the wash baskets we went and layered them with blankets. They both sat in their little nests pretending to be little chicks whilst I fed them worms (breakfast). We then made up a story about a mommy bird building a nest for her eggs and waiting for them to hatch. This all tied in with the baby we were waiting for as I was thirty-six weeks pregnant.

This is just one example of a heart-warming experience I had the joy of having with my kids when I took advantage of an opportunity. This does not occur every day for even if the opportunity arises, the timing may not be right. If it did happen every day it may not have the special impact it does have when it occurs naturally. Also, my kids would be expecting it to happen all the time which can lead to other problems. However when the timing is right and the opportunity naturally arises, it is magical and it also helps my children to be more aware of the environment around them, which is a life skill in itself.

A helping hand of kindness

During the past few years I have grown to appreciate more the kindness that some people express so naturally. I have experienced it more since moving to Australia. It has renewed my faith in humankind and every time it has happened it has been a woman who has touched my soul so kindly like an angel sent to shine a light out of the darkness. There are a lot of kind women out there who are totally unselfish and who are probably not aware how much of a positive impact that they are having on others by simply taking that one moment out of time to consider someone in need.

The first time it happened was when I was thirty-six weeks pregnant with my third child. We had migrated to Australia from Ireland a few days before and had just booked into a chalet in a holiday park. It was raining and I was sitting in the park with my boys when a woman in her early fifties approached me to ask if I would like a television for the boys. Her way of asking was as if I was doing her a favour by taking it. I accepted it and we chatted for a while. Even though she didn't know the area, she educated me about Australia and what to expect and she told me about her children growing up in Australia. She reassured me, which is exactly what I needed to hear as I was sitting watching my boys, hoping I had done the right thing by migrating. She was such a positive influence and inspiration and our meeting was much more than about a television. I never saw her again and I so wish I could tell her how much she helped me.

The second time was after my baby was born. She was six weeks old and I started going to a local playgroup. I didn't know anyone in Australia and I knew it would take a while to get to know people. I met a lady one day and she was so kind to everyone in the group and to all of the children. We got chatting and hit it off straight away and we exchanged numbers so as to arrange a play date for the kids. Imagine how vulnerable I was at this time, all alone in a new country. She took me under her wing and also educated me on how things went in Australia. She never once made me feel like a hindrance and she seemed genuinely fascinated about how things differed between life here and Ireland and made me feel interesting again. We are still friends and I value her friendship so much.

The third time was when I was in the supermarket. My son was playing up a little and he was in a double pushchair with his sister. I was trying to gather a few bits and pieces and I wasn't really myself as I was in the early stages of pregnancy and still feeling quite ill. Instead of taking the buggy across the path of oncoming trolleys, I ran across myself and got a carton of strawberry milk for my son. To my horror I heard a crash and crying. My darling son had decided to hop out of the buggy, only to make it uneven so that it flipped back with my daughter in it. A woman in her forties immediately lifted it up as I held my son's hand and she tried to reassure my daughter, who was crying because a strange woman had lifted the buggy. I thanked the woman and I was in a fluster and she looked at me calmly and said, "Don't you worry about it, I was there myself too." Those few words sank right in and refocused me. I no longer felt anxious and not in control. I would love that beautiful lady to know that her random act of kindness really was appreciated and made a big difference to me.

I now try my best to take the time to slow the pace and be more considerate. So what if I am a bit late or don't get something done? It is not the end of the world. I know I can make little positive changes in the world by reaching out and touching those in a moment of need. I would love to think that something I have done has touched someone for a moment. Imagine if we all took a few moments to consider others and to hold out a helping hand unconditionally when a stranger was in need. Would the world not be a better place?

Conscious minds

An amazing realisation was gifted to me by a dear friend. I have always been of the understanding that many of our mental health issues are caused due to chemical imbalances in the brain. This preconception is due to working within the mental health sector for almost four years. I never challenged the information provided to me. I accepted that for any of us who encounter a time of mental instability, the best thing to restore the balance is by incorporating medicine to ensure the individual returns to a more socially acceptable state of being in as short a time as possible.

But is this the way it is supposed to be? Or is this the easy way out by suppressing the emergence of our spiritual enlightenment?

My friend challenged my views and took the time to offer me a different understanding that immediately seemed so natural and logical. It was one of those 'Aha' moments that Oprah often goes on about. Another missing piece of my puzzle of knowing has been discovered.

What did she tell you? I hear you ask. She said there is now evidence that depression is not a chemical imbalance in the brain but a spiritual emergence most of the time. Some people are not ready for this and so through fear they visit their doctor to stop the process through prescribed medication. That is akin to taking a tablet to get rid of a temperature when the body has a temperature to get rid of infection. If all of these emergences were dealt with through love, care and support, people would be able to go through the process naturally and get back to their lives with a better understanding of themselves without becoming dependant on prescription drugs for many years. As you can see, my friend is very wise.

"Most people often find themselves trying to logically explain spiritual nudges that come to them. The thing about allowing our intellectual mind to reason things away is that we often miss out on some blessings and important information."
Kunbikorostensky embracingchanges.com

We are moving forward into a new era, one of collective consciousness. Those who do not embrace this transition will be left behind. Humanity is evolving. The way things have been will be no more. Since time began there have been many stages of evolution within the dominant species. Things cannot stay the same forever. Look at the era of the dinosaurs. They started walking the earth two hundred and fifty million years ago and approximately every fifty million years after that they evolved to a different stage of being from the Triassic period to the Jurassic period and then to the Cretaceous period around one hundred and forty six million years ago.

Fortunately we are not dramatically evolving physically, but as with other times during humanity's reign on this Earth we are experiencing a shift in consciousness. One time in history that is significant and universally familiar is the coming of Jesus. He changed the consciousness of humanity; he provided people with a more pure line of thought that spread across the world thousands of years before globalisation. A more positive inner thinking mindset is what is shining through and being embraced by many enlightened individuals since. Can you imagine today one person having so much influence on the entire population of the world?

As we often bring forth with us the views and beliefs of our parents and their parents and their parents, and so on, all having an influence in how we perceive things during our lifetime, many of us are finding it challenging to allow the spirit to shine through. These changes do not feel 'normal' for so many of us and they can generate a very unsettling feeling. If we are not aware of our own being during this time it can be quite disturbing and this in turn can lead us to seek help from the person many of us have been taught can make everything better, our GP. This of course assists with shielding a patient from experiencing the unsettling feelings they are not ready to fully embrace.

In my experience it is through embracing these emotions and dealing with them at a more conscious level that we are able to move forward into a more fulfilling and connected state of being.

My Story

About five years ago everything I knew to be changed for me. It was after having my second son and I was getting on with life as a new mum again. One night my brother and my boyfriend had a fight. It wasn't that I was never used to witnessing a punch up, but this time I bore the emotional scars of the event. It shook me to my core, maybe because I was a little more emotionally vulnerable at the time, or maybe because I was ready to go within to discover the gifts I had.

I never pursued getting any medical assistance as I knew what was happening to me and I wasn't afraid. I knew I had to take it one day at a time, which is the same for any trauma. When I needed to talk, I did. My body guided me through the recovery process. I connected with myself at a higher level and in moments of need I discovered that I could make decisions I could not have made before.

As time passed it became much easier to function. My thoughts came together and a feeling of knowing engulfed me. This feeling is a wonderful sensation that is both physically relaxing and psychologically satisfying. To know I am on the right track and that I am being guided by myself is wondrous. I am becoming increasingly aware and full of insightful wisdom.

Had I not experienced my time of distress I believe I would not be living as fulfilling a life as I am and I know that I will be for eternity.

One thing I know for sure is that our conscious minds are not to be feared. If allowed to grow naturally, an increased vastness of open consciousness that has the potential to spread across the globe will guide humanity towards a more fulfilling existence. Harmony and peace may prevail.

"Throughout the harrowing times in life comes the opportunity to grow, as often we seek solace from within. It is through fear that progress towards enlightenment stalls or is suppressed. After the struggle comes the breakthrough."

Here's a thought: Maybe many of those who are diagnosed with having 'mental health problems' are actually going through a personal transition to a more spiritually enlightened state of being. And maybe what they need to help them survive through this time is not medication, which prevents the person from moving on from the struggle to the more fulfilling stage of the breakthrough. By offering healing love, positive energy and guidance, most people have the potential to progress towards a more fulfilling experience of life. I like to think of it as a 'Heaven on Earth' type of existence.

If someone is experiencing depression or has feelings of unease or uncertainty or even an unsettling change of behaviour, why not treat them with the love, support and compassion that we instinctively express when we encounter someone who is experiencing grief. This type of response is what helps bring a person through the harrowing experience of losing a loved one. Why could the same response not work for someone who is experiencing a mental challenge? There is no longer any room for negative responses such as judgment and fear in our societies if we hope to move forward to a more harmonious future together.

Loving energy is a true healer—let it shine.

Go within or go without

One of the best things I have ever done in life is to go within. Since doing this a whole new treasure trove of wisdom and fulfilment has found me. Don't get me wrong, I still encounter life's challenges from time to time, but they now don't seem as challenging because I am in the knowing that no matter what happens, it is more than likely happening for a greater good in the long run.

I know for a fact that when I am on a frequency of happiness and contentment, more happiness and contentment comes my way. Every now and again I may put a request out there for something I desire and then I do nothing other than act on the opportunities that present themselves to me. The universe is in motion, bringing to me whatever it is that I have requested. This is not always a good thing because if I truly feel and believe that something not so good is going to happen, then that will find me also. Also it is worth bearing in mind that we must be careful what we wish for as the sacrifices we may have to make to make way for the delivery of the desire may not be worth it in the end.

However sometimes negatives happen to make way for more positives. Or maybe sometimes we are being tested by a messenger to receive a gift bigger and better than your everyday requests.

Going within does not necessarily have anything to do with religion, although many people use religion as a vehicle to guide them through the tough times and to send off more frequencies of happiness, thus attracting more joyous moments. It is logical when you think about it. Also, positive energies combined are very powerful. For the greater good of humanity, if more and more groups come together with the aspiration of positivity, then positive things will happen.

Others may access meditation for a more connected, intense experience. Stillness and an empty mind help cleanse the soul and get rid of the entire toxic gunk that has accumulated there over time. A poem by Jodi Davis sums it up in a few short but inspiring words.

Go within or go without
by Jodi Davis
Life is a school with one lesson to learn
a major in Love is what I'm talking about.
You won't find it out there in the desert
You must go within or go without.
We spend years crawling in dry sands
scorched by the desert's burning heat.
Until we look inside our hearts
we're left yearning for something we can't see.
Fed by an ego afraid of being forgotten
it whispers that it knows the way
When you turn from the voice of ego
Love reminds you, you're already safe.
You can only discover the sweet embrace of Love
through learning to love your Self.
Then you will find it easy to begin
now you are free to love everybody else.
We are all "one" in reality
when you find pure Love you'll have No Doubt.
Yet you can make this discovery only one way
you must go within or go without.

Another thing that I discovered when I went within was forgiveness. This I discovered and embraced as it is truly a gift to me and no one else. Through forgiveness I have opened so many doors that I had shut over the years and it gives me a glow inside when I think about it so I know that forgiveness is good for me.

The Glow

The glow is like my spiritual guide. It lets me know when I am making the right decision. It can be mistaken for excitement but when you learn to recognise the glow it will be an invaluable way of being guided by your spirit. I have realised that this is what Jesus was talking about when he referred to the Holy Spirit. As a child I used to think it was a dove with a shining light beaming behind it sort of experience, but I now know that this is an inner glow guiding us through life and must be respected and listened to if we wish to travel the right path for us in life.

Love

Love is divine, love is healing, and love is all powerful. I could go on all day about love. It frees us to connect with others. When we open our heart chakra we are inviting and sharing ourselves with others, which I believe to be the true path to fulfilment. When we feel true love for another it is healing. Have you ever thought about why a mummy kiss is all healing? I know I have, us mums pump so much love into that kiss that it actually helps our children heal. I never cease to be amazed at the power of this healing love. When we believe and the child believes that all will be well then it will, because no fear or doubt is harboured. I feel that this also applies to all aspects of healing and life in general. We all have the ability to heal and be healed through divine love and unwavering belief.

Strength

When I say strength I don't mean the physical type, I am thinking more of strength of character. Because we are human we all have strengths and weaknesses, that's what makes us interesting. Strength comes from within and helps us through tough challenges that we all face at some time or other throughout life. It is our strength that keeps us sane and keeps us filled with hope and trust that all will get easier and that life is good, even though it may not feel that way sometimes. It is our strength that helps us bounce back, maybe even wiser than before we stumbled.

Inspiration

We all have a creative side. When we don't express our creativity in the way that is unique to us all then we will find it hard to ever be fulfilled. For me creativity comes in the form of writing and drawing, I just love expressing myself this way. Other people use music, sports and other mediums as a vehicle of self expression. But all in all, it comes from the same creative source within to begin with and just a different avenue is explored to express it. The world would be a boring place if we all expressed our creativity in the same way, wouldn't it? I like to think of creative expression as the rainbow that beams right around the world sprinkling droplets of love and hope and happiness and making way for the sun to shine.

An affirmation found me when I was in the middle of writing this article and it encompasses the essence of what I feel.

"I allow myself to trust in the process of life and what I need comes to me easily and effortlessly."

My advice if you want to go within is, don't force it. It will happen naturally when you are ready. You need to slow down and listen to yourself. Don't have miraculous expectations in your mind. My experience is more of everything clicking together and a feeling of safety and awareness. So don't forget: Go within or go without.

Positive thinking

Have you ever stopped to think that there could be another reason for your brain other than storing and processing information, for decision making and making our bodies function? Our brain is the control centre of our bodies and its capabilities can be somewhat underestimated. Take a moment to consider the possibility that your brain could not only be used to make your body complete tasks such as walking or talking or for storing information, but that your mind has the possibility to be unlocked, enabling you to heal yourself mentally and physically simply by feeling more positive.

By exploring the fact that our body sends out signals that we generate within ourselves, and that our body is like a magnet therefore it attracts the same signals back, I have discovered the advantages of positive thinking. I have always been a very optimistic person, always believing that anything is possible and the only barrier in the way of achieving anything I wanted to achieve was myself, so I am a willing subject.

"You are an electromagnetic being emitting a frequency. Only those things that are on the same frequency as the one you are emitting can come into your experience. Every single person, event, and circumstance in your day is telling you what frequency you are on. If your day is not going well, stop and deliberately change your frequency. If your day is going swimmingly, keep doing what you are doing." Rhonda Byrne

We sometimes put petitions in place stopping us from seeing any further. I was always a healthy person and I never had any health problems. I went through a rough patch in my life for a few years and my optimism ended up being the main casualty. I didn't trust my thoughts any more, I didn't listen to my little voice of intuition that I had always relied on to lead me in the right direction. I couldn't make decisions confidently as I lost confidence in my decision-making abilities.

During this time I suffered from really aggressive gum disease so bad that my teeth started to fall apart. The bone in my jaw is wasting away and unable to support my teeth for much longer. I am also in a lot of pain and my mouth is on fire a lot of the time. The reason I share my ailment with you is because I have discovered how powerful the mind is to help us heal ourselves. I was given Louise L Hay's book *You can heal your life* by a beautiful friend. I have been awakened to a different perspective. My mouth had reached the point that I could barely talk, it hurt so much. I read what it said about teeth and gums and realised that the probable cause given in the book was so right for my circumstances. I started saying the recommended affirmations and within a few days the pain was nowhere near as intense.

Some eye openers from Louise L Hay:

- What we think about ourselves becomes the truth for us. I believe that everyone, myself included, is responsible for everything in our lives, the best and the worst.

- Learn to think in positive affirmations...Continually make positive statements about how you want your life to be. Do it in the present tense.
- No matter what the problem, the main issue is LOVING THE SELF. This is the 'magic wand' that dissolves problems.
- Your mind is a tool for you to use in any way you wish...the thoughts you 'choose' to think create the experiences you have.
- The question 'Is it true or real?' has two answers. 'Yes' and 'No'. It is true if you believe it to be true. It is not true if you believe it isn't true.
- Self-approval and self-acceptance in the now are the keys to positive changes.

By combining positive thinking with medical assistance, recovery times can be significantly shortened. We often hear of people who have 'miraculous recoveries' and how their positive attitude helped them to stay focused on their recovery, only to shock the medical practitioners who were assisting them. It is that powerful.

Another way of looking at positive thinking is that a lot of us spend our lives chasing a dream, searching for the perfect job or the perfect love story, but what if we stopped searching? What if we changed our thinking and allowed ourselves to feel like we had it already, therefore sending out signals from our body which will attract that one thing we have searched for to come and find us. This type of thinking reminds me of a little story introduced to me by two wonderful friends.

"There was a little girl who was out searching for ladybirds one day. She searched and searched and could not find any. Eventually she fell asleep on the grass and dreamed of ladybirds. When she woke up she was covered in ladybirds."

It is only when we stop looking and start feeling that things are drawn to us.

American researcher Dan Buettner, who has researched many lifestyles throughout the world, has discovered that religious people who are great positive thinkers and believers in their faith have higher levels of wellbeing and can add anywhere between four to fourteen years to their lives. He says there are four domains to a longer life:

1. Move naturally: Find ways to move mindlessly, make moving unavoidable.
2. Right outlook: An important component in longevity – know your purpose and slow down.
3. Eat wisely: You can gain eight extra years. Tips – stop when eighty per cent full/eat more plants/drink red wine.
4. Connect: Belonging to the right group of healthy-minded, supportive people might be the most powerful thing you can do to change your lifestyle for the better.

All in all, what have we got to lose? Nothing! But we certainly have a lot to gain from being more positive and open to changing our perspective on life. We can potentially create a better sense of wellbeing for ourselves, which can rub off on those around us in a positive way.

We also have the added bonus of adding years to our lives. So what are we all waiting for – let's get positive. It doesn't cost a cent yet it could be the best investment you will ever make.

The Push

Throughout life I have come to learn that sometimes in order to achieve or get over the line with a certain task we need to push ourselves that little bit more than usual to achieve optimum results. Consider moving house, having a baby, graduating from a course, getting married—these are all seen as significant events in an individual's life.

I thought about this when I moved house. I was settled and content in my old house but a shift in my thoughts left me feeling unsettled and I felt that a change for the best was needed. Luckily it has been a good move for us but it has certainly come with a lot of 'pushing'. Packing, de-cluttering, cleaning and organising for two adults and four children were just a few of the tasks I took upon myself to complete in a short time. 'Is it any wonder it is said that moving house is one of the most stressful events in anyone's lifetime,' I thought, then laughed. I remembered that only three years earlier I had packed up, de-cluttered and organised for me and my family to move to the other side of the world without giving much thought to the enormity of the pursuit ahead—and all this whilst I was heavily pregnant.

I was also reminded that in a three-year time frame not too long beforehand I had moved five times, albeit with one child in tow not four, but still quite an upheaval. Why? Looking back I know I was in pursuit of happiness, although I would not have admitted that at the time. Since coming to Australia I have become more settled and content with all aspects of my life and I no longer feel the urge to push as much as I did. I let things find me or act on creative urges as and when they come and it all feels so natural and right. I look back to where I was in life a few years ago. I hated the word 'content'. For me that word was weak and one thing I did not want to be perceived as was weak. I pushed and pushed every day of my life and I was exceeding myself quite regularly. I know now that it was all part of my journey and I am happy to have experienced every blood pumping moment of it but now 'contentment' is a word I embrace and 'pushing' is what I do when it needs to be done and I am happy doing it. For me now there is less stress in my life, a win-win scenario.

The unavoidable push

Giving birth is a prime example of when pushing yourself you can receive maximum results. What I can only describe as intense moments of pushing have produced the most beautiful and wonderful of all of life's gifts straight to me. What I have taken from these experiences as I have endured them is that when I am calm and organised with my thoughts and relaxed, things flowed naturally as they should. It was then that the job was done in half the time. I reckon this theory can be addressed to every aspect of life.

Pushy people

Be grateful for the people that push your buttons and work your nerves. They're teaching you a lesson and serving a purpose in your life.

There are those who push with good intentions and those who don't. They both may hold the key to personal development but the issue arising may be that it is not development of choice, it is one of force and therefore it may feel uncomfortable to the person being pushed. However, when I feel like this I always remind myself that through conflict comes the potential for positive change and this strengthens me to progress forward.

P.U.S.H

The following story found me when I was writing this article and I thought it gave a new refreshing thought process to the word PUSH.

Push for Life!
A man was sleeping in his cabin when suddenly his room was filled with light, and God appeared. The Lord told the man he had work for him to do, and showed him a large rock in front of his cabin.

The Lord explained that the man was to push against the rock with all his might. So, this the man did, day after day.

For many days he toiled from sun up to sun down, his shoulders set squarely against the cold massive surface of the unmoving rock, pushing with all his might. Each night the man returned to his cabin sore and worn out, feeling that his whole day had been spent in vain.

Since the man was showing discouragement, the Adversary (Satan) decided to enter the picture by placing thoughts into the weary mind: "You have been pushing against that rock for a long time, and it hasn't moved."

Thus, he gave the impression that the task was impossible and that he was a failure. These thoughts discouraged and disheartened the man.

Satan said, "Why kill yourself over this? Just put in your time, giving just the minimum effort; and that will be good enough."

That's what the weary man planned to do, but decided to make it a matter of prayer and to take his troubled thoughts to the Lord.

"Lord," he said. "I have laboured long and hard in your service, putting all my strength to do that which you have asked. Yet, after all this time, I have not even budged that rock by half a millimetre. What is wrong? Why am I failing?"

The Lord responded compassionately, "My friend, when I asked you to serve me and you accepted, I told you to push against the rock with all of your strength, which you have done. Never once did I mention to you that I expected you to move it.

"Your task was to push. And now you come to me with your strength spent, thinking that you have failed. But is that really so?

"Through opposition you have grown much, and your abilities now surpass that which you used to have.

"Look at yourself. Your arms are strong and muscled, your back sinewy and brown: your hands are

callused from constant pressure, your legs have become massive and hard.

"Now I, my friend, will move the rock. True, you haven't moved the rock. But your calling was to be obedient and to push and to exercise your faith and trust in My Wisdom. That you have done."

At times when we hear a word from God, we tend to use our own intellect to decipher what He wants, when usually what God wants is just a simple obedience and faith in him. By all means exercise the faith that moves mountains, but know that it is still God who moves mountains.

When everything seems to go wrong just P.U.S.H

When the job gets you down just P.U.S.H

When people don't react the way you think they should just P.U.S.H

When your money is gone and the bills are due just P.U.S.H

When people just don't understand you just P.U.S.H

P=Pray
U=Until
S=Something
H=Happens

Pushing is all part of life. As children we push ourselves and others continuously to determine where our boundaries are, which enables us to develop physically and emotionally. Being more mindful of when we push and possibly simplifying why we push may mean that we become more aware of ourselves and others.

Take a moment to understand when and why in your life that you have experienced pushing.

Are we responsible for the effect we have on others?

Are you the type of person that treads through life carefully? Not wanting to upset anyone or make anyone feel uneasy?

In this diverse world with so many people with different it is virtually impossible to get through life without upsetting some of them no matter how nice we try to be.

I believe the answer to the question in the title has a lot to do with intention. If we are true to ourselves and conduct our day to day interactions with others with the truest of intentions then we cannot possibly be held accountable for the responses of others. If they respond negatively then that will be to do with their own life learning, the influences of family and other choices they have made during their existence. It will be the responsibility of the other person to gift themselves with the understanding of why they react in such a way to the comment or action.

However, if I intentionally set out to purposely offend or hurt the feelings of another, then yes, I am in some way responsible for any subsequent action. I say 'in some way' because we are all individually accountable for how we react to others.

Then again, what if as a writer I have a negative effect on someone who has read something I have written, am I responsible? Does it fall under the same category as a one on one interaction? All I know is that I write as I speak, which is with the truest of intentions, and that I only ever write to help others or share my experiences and thoughts and in that I hope the answer is clear.

I have beautiful friends who take ownership of the feelings of others when they consider they have instigated a reaction they did not intend to happen. I know they have not set out to make anyone feel bad but in being their beautiful selves they want to fix it and make the scenario right again. I have come to realise that in some scenarios it is OK to make amends so that the other person knows you are sorry you made them feel sad or angry or whatever emotion the reaction brought to light. But on the whole it must be considered that by being true to ourselves it has brought up something the other person clearly needs to work on for their own self progression. If they are deprived of the opportunity to learn these lessons through their feelings being protected by another, then it is a pity because the life lesson will keep cropping up. Friendships may be deprived of becoming more fulfilling or in they may drag on when they are clearly not supposed to.

How we perceive something will determine how we approach it, therefore influencing our interactions with others. If you are not happy with the way something you are doing is affecting others, why not change your thoughts about the process? If we approach something from a more positive mindset then we not only alter our own experiences of it, we will also alter our interactions with others who experience our energy. This can be applied to everything we do, from playing with our children to doing the shopping, to going to work or out for the night.

Let's take it to another level and consider the metaphysics of it all. Our thoughts create energy and when our energy is solemn or happy or angry or uncaring, other people who come in contact with us will pick up on those vibes we are sending out into the world. I think of it as our glow. When I am happy my glow is beaming and attracting wonderful things and people my way. When I am sad I am attracting sadness. When I am ill I attract more illness. When I am fearful I attract more things to be fearful about. The list goes on but it all comes down to us being magnetic. Of course there are people we choose to be with that may not be attracted to us just because of the energy we are emitting and so their energy and mine will entwine. They may complement each other right in that moment or they may clash but if we are aware of it then we can adjust to the scenario should we wish to do so. All in all, the answer is that we can have a huge influence on how we affect others through being aware of our thoughts and energy.

We have the potential to affect others through all of our actions during each and every day, whether we choose to be aware of it or not. When we gift ourselves with awareness of how others react to us and when we become a little more courteous during our interactions, we will often discover that we have more positive encounters. Of course some people do not appreciate kindness and in this scenario it is up to us if we choose to continue interactions. Being more aware can assist in how you are remembered and also how you experience others.

"It is not always what you say that others will remember, it is how you made them feel."

Some people choose not to be conscious of their effects on others and this may be because they cannot deal with the responsibility that comes hand in hand with being true to ourselves and how that may affect others. Sometimes these people may choose to isolate and detach themselves from people they could potentially encounter, but this may be because they have to work on themselves before they can become responsible for the effects they have on another.

We do influence each other when we interact, whether we choose to take personal responsibility for each communication or not, no matter how big or small. The energy we are sending out can make a difference to the atmosphere of conversations, which can add to or take away from the moment. But I would like to turn the question around and ask,

'Would you hold someone else accountable for how you react to them?'

Forgiving spirit

"When we realise the power of forgiveness, our spirit is reborn."

Forgiveness can be a complex subject for most of us to deal with. When we are wronged and face injustice it is natural for our human spirit to become consumed with resentment. This resentment does more harm to the resentful person than it does to the perpetrator.

If you love yourself you will be able to free yourself from the chains that connect you to this negative source.

Forgiveness is hard to find when someone is not remorseful for their actions, but in order to free yourself from the negative connection to that person's energy or the situation itself, you can always forgive from afar. This will free you from any association.

Forgiveness and grief

In the situation of someone you love being taken for you it is human nature to seek a reason and someone to blame. This will give us an avenue to release external anger and sadness. Forgiveness has a big part to play in healing and moving on in this instance. Many people choose to stay in the resentment and sadness that consumes them during this time because the pain is so intense. But it is those of us who find the courage to go within, honor our grief and heal our broken hearts who will be able to move forward, choosing to keep the beauty of the life they lost alive within them instead of the alternative. Our bodies and minds have been equipped to deal with grief as it is part of life. We must not block it out.

Self forgiveness

My experience of forgiveness touches on many parts of my life and on different levels. I have always had a forgiving nature and that in a way is a good thing, but when someone is purposefully doing something to get to you it can be dangerous to forgive too easily. My problem with forgiveness was not with forgiving another, it was to do with forgiving myself.

Maybe I expected too much from others to forgive me when I did things wrong as I would have moved on with my life and forgiven them without batting an eyelid. But it wasn't until my spirit guided me to address each of my misgivings that I realised I had not moved on in the way I thought I had. Each of those times that I hurt someone and charged forward without a care in the world, I had not stopped to consider how my actions had affected another. Nor had I considered forgiving myself or even, as a Catholic, seeking forgiveness through confessions.

The consequence of this was that a few years ago I experienced a very deep time when I was made to relive each of the occurrences in my dreams. I felt all of the emotions this time around and it was so real, even more real than the first time I had experienced it. I wondered what to do. Should I contact each person I had made feel bad and apologise for my actions? I am quite sure all those boyfriends I dumped have moved on in their lives and wouldn't want an ex-girlfriend popping back i just so that she could rid herself of guilt. No, I knew this was not an option at the time as I hadn't long had a child and people would think I had gone crazy. I came to the conclusion that I needed to have more of an acceptance of my past and everything that has made me the person I am today.

I decided to forgive myself for everything I felt needed to be addressed and I sent positive loving energy to each of the people I felt I had hurt. In doing this I honoured each lesson I have learned, and understood what every person that came into my life has done to help me come to this point of realisation. I too came into their lives for the same reason. Everyone is a positive or negative part of someone's life but it is all part of the process and acceptance is a big part.

As for letting those people know that I am sorry, well I trust that if and when the time is right, the opportunity will find me. Now that I am in the knowing I will not waste those opportunities. The world works in mysterious ways and there is no such thing as circumstance, everything happens for a reason.

Now that I live myself in total forgiveness my heart is more open. Wisdom comes flooding to me when I need it. I am closer to my inner guide, who directs me towards fulfilling my heart's desires. This has all happened because I can forgive. Forgiveness is not a gift to someone else, it is a gift to yourself.

Reasoning

It is easier to forgive another when we realise that everyone who crosses our path during our lifetime has done so for a reason. As we experience different experiences both good and bad, we grow a little more. We become more knowledgeable and our spirit grows.

What would your life be like today if you chose to forgive someone who caused you be unforgiving? Does the negative energy that is created because of the captured resentment weigh you down at times? Should you choose to forgive, it will feel like a great weight has been lifted off your shoulders and your spirit will feel free again.

"When we realise the power of forgiveness, our spirit is reborn."

Personal evolution: To become a butterfly?

I once watched a David Attenborough wildlife program that showed the life cycle of a caterpillar. Not just an ordinary caterpillar; this caterpillar lived in Siberia, where it was only sunny for a short period of the year and icy cold the rest.

The caterpillar would go around munching as much as it could all day long. It would munch, munch, munch. Then suddenly, before it got to the cocoon stage the cold and ice came and the caterpillar froze. Amazingly, when the sun came and the ice melted the caterpillar would come alive again and continue munching and munching and munching again in a desperate bid to eat a sufficient amount so it could reach the stage where it became a cocoon. But alas, this year was not to be its year either, and the big frost came and the caterpillar froze again. Many cycles came and went and the caterpillar never lost faith that one day it would reach the stage at which it could find its sanctuary in the cocoon. So it continued to munch, munch, munch until finally one year, before the ice came it turned into a cocoon and spared itself from another deep freezing. That year it became a butterfly and was able to fly to wherever it wanted to go.

It got me thinking and when I made a connection between the caterpillar's quest and the quest that many of us humans pursue, I was intrigued. I thought about how many of us keep munching and munching but give up before we reap the fruits of our labour. The caterpillar had faith, one hundred per cent belief, absolute unwavering knowing that it would make it, and against all the odds it did. It may take many attempts but if we keep following our instinct then we will get there.

Those people who are willing to work hard and persevere by weathering the storms are rewarded, especially when we follow our heart. That little caterpillar followed its heart; it so wanted to reach its goal and it instinctively knew how to get there. It is not as if it attended caterpillar school and was taught how to do it; no, it instinctively knew how to move forward, what it needed to do.

We will all get many opportunities to evolve during our lifetimes; we are ever changing beings. Some people choose to experience their life as only a caterpillar but those who listen to their inner guide and move towards enlightenment by following their heart's desire will feel what it is like to live in the beauty and freedom that is being a beautiful butterfly.

Yes, to become a butterfly you must work hard, however you will be guided through the process and before you emerge in all your glory you will have some time in your cocoon to rest, contemplate and prepare yourself for your new coming.

Are you a butterfly or are you content with being a caterpillar? Whatever path you choose, remember that the butterfly knows what it is like to be a caterpillar but the caterpillar does not yet know what it is like to be a butterfly. 1300 views and published.

Embracing the Butterfly
Being a mum in business

So you have been treading along munching away not fully knowing what the outcome is going to be, your only certainty being an inner belief that what you are doing is what you have to do in order to make something magical happen. Every leaf is an opportunity to grow. Sometimes the leaves are scattered and you have to work harder to find them and other times they just fall before you. You instinctively know that you just have to keep moving forward with gusto in this unwavering belief in order to build up that reserve for your business, just like the caterpillar instinctively knows that he has to keep munching those leaves without fully knowing what the outcome is going to be a mum in business must trust that she is making the right choices and building up her reserve tank in order to grow bigger and better than before.

The caterpillar does not know at this point that it will become a butterfly as far as it is concerned it may just end up being a fat caterpillar. It is the magic of the inner knowing that something wonderful will happen, but yet not fully knowing, that makes the caterpillar's journey spectacular.

It takes courage to keep going and often life and circumstance can hold you back but you have the choice to charge ahead walking your own path in the knowing that something amazing can happen if you just keep pushing forward.

Then it happens, the day finally comes when things start to change. You may not feel quite yourself as a huge transition begins to occur. This is the time to take a step back and let things happen. You need to do nothing but wait. It is time to gather your energy as you are growing wings. You may not know what they are for yet but you rest, even reflect on all of the hard work you have put in.

Then it happens. The day comes when the cocoon opens and you are ready to squeeze out into the world. Bright, colourful and majestic you open your wings and fly. You cannot fully see your true splendor but you know that something wondrous has just happened and you must now fly.

Take a moment to consider that the caterpillar has no knowledge of how to fly as it has always had its feet firmly planted on the ground. Yet when it embraces that specific moment when it is disembarking from its hideaway. Magic happens.

The moral of this story is that every caterpillar has no clue when it starts out that it has the potential to become a butterfly, it only has an inner knowing that it must keep eating and one day when the time is right something wonderful will happen.

'A caterpillar does not know what it is like to be a butterfly; a butterfly appreciates what it is like to be a caterpillar.'

When we start out in business we do not fully know what the outcome is going to be. We can plan, we can navigate the path as best we can but the outcome comes from a higher source.

'When time and circumstance align, magic happens'

You too can be a business butterfly if you believe.

What do you choose for yourself today?

Making choices can be difficult for some people. Maybe because we have so many options open to us all in this day and age and many of us fear not making the right decision. Most people know that it is the choices we make in the now that manifest and determine our future. That can seem quite overwhelming for many of us, me included.

I have been known to be indecisive at times; but when I make up my mind to do something I do all in my power to complete that task, to my peril at times but also to my advantage. I go with my gut instinct as much as I can because then I am always in the knowing that I am making the choices that feel right for me. I have learned to trust that my internal spirit will guide me, especially through the tough times. It is comforting to know I have a helping hand when I need it most.

When we make the right choices for us it helps us to grow spiritually.

Looking back I realise that it is when I went against my intuition as my ego took centre stage that I chose to go ahead when actually I should have retracted. These instances were not a total waste of my precious time, they were all part of my journey through life, and I have learned as much from my mistakes as I have from the successes.

> *"It is fine to make mistakes, once we learn from them and don't keep repeating them."*

This is something my parents told me as I was growing up. They would always forgive me the first time I did something wrong but if I kept repeating the same mistakes over and again, well then I needed them to intervene and guide me.

Why do we fear making choices?

Is it because through our choices change occurs? Change can be something to fear for so many, because on many occasions it cannot be fully controlled. It is human nature to want to control everything because we want to protect ourselves and those we love from being hurt. It is not a bad trait but it can block a lot of goodness from finding us.

I have often experienced difficulties in making decisions, especially when my choices affect others. Any choice that I make directly affects those closest to me. I have however come to a solution for me. I now trust in my instinct to guide me. By allowing my spirit to help me make the decision that is right for me then I am keeping myself on track. When I am on my right path for me then those closest to me benefit because I am able to provide them with the best of me.

Empowering choices

We make conscious and unconscious choices all the time. When we choose to navigate ourselves towards positivity then we can often discover we are empowering ourselves.

Every morning at buildingbeautifulbonds.com we were given the opportunity to express what we choose for ourselves today. In my experience this small yet powerful technique is very successful in facilitating a positive mindset that grows throughout the day. When we start our day on the right note it is easier to maintain a happier attitude to life and if we are all truly honest with ourselves, happiness is what we are all striving towards in life. Simplicity is bliss, empowerment helps us grow.

Difficult choices

Often when we are faced with making difficult decisions many of us really don't want the responsibility. This is only natural because if we were to make a choice and the outcome was not positive, we would be to blame. Many people avoid taking risks, which ensures they are never held accountable for any wrong decisions. However, it is all right to make the wrong decisions sometimes as it helps us to learn valuable lessons and ensures we keep growing.

When you are experiencing difficulty making choices, I suggest you find a quiet space, relax, close your eyes and allow yourself to listen to what your instinct is trying to tell you. What outcome can you honestly say you could live with? Our inner spirit is there to guide us when we face difficulties in life.

"When we allow ourselves to trust in the universe, from the greatest despair can come the greatest gift."

Here are some of my tips for making choices easier.

1. Listen to your inner guide. If you find this difficult there are many mediums that can assist you to access this energy.
2. Let your first choice of every day be to approach each decision with the right attitude.
3. Instead of seeking blame, seek a solution.
4. Trust that every choice you make is contributing to your greater good, even if it doesn't seem so at the time.
5. Choose to be grateful.

Accept that our choices, good and bad, are all contributing to who we are right now and that even if we have made the wrong choices in the past that doesn't mean we have to keep making wrong choices for us. No, that just means we have the opportunity to make a u-turn and begin moving towards a happier path.

Every day is a new beginning and when we choose to begin our day by making the choice to have a more positive attitude then we are giving ourselves and those closest to us the best start to every day.

Awakening

"An act or moment of becoming suddenly aware of something." dictionary.com

I am privileged in life to know that I have personally awakened spiritually. I cannot imagine how my life would have ever felt fully fulfilled without this and I feel blessed to have discovered this gift. For me it is not all about religion, even though I believe religion has a huge place in the world, socially, for a greater good.

Personally, my awakening has been about the missing pieces of the puzzle of life slotting into place and everything seems so much clearer. I now see things from a wider spectrum that I have always known was there, but chose not to experience. I have realised that by having total faith and belief in whatever it is that means the most to me at any given time, is sufficient to enable me to receive. If it is within the power of the universe to provide the answer for me, it will. If it is for my greater good it will find me.

Awakening my soul has left me with a sense of understanding. This feeling that I refer to as 'knowing' is very powerful. And if the Laws of Attraction are to be truly believed then only beautiful things will come my way as beauty and love is what I feel most.

Simplicity

One of the most fascinating entities of the whole process which I discovered is that life is not as complicated as we all make it out to be. It is all quite simple actually. I understand it to be like this: We are all energy, every single thing living on this planet Earth is energy. We have magnetic fields that surround us and attract to us what we vibrate. SIMPLE. By believing that something is as it is, we feel that it is already and so attract more of that belief to us. What we truly allow ourselves to believe is what we truly allow ourselves to experience.

Connection

I now feel a deeper connection to God. I understand and truly believe that miracles can and do happen in this beautiful world of ours. I believe that messengers and truly inspirational people are gifts sent to us from God, helping us to find our way to inner peace, because when we awaken to inner peace then we are best placed to help others find theirs. The more people that become peaceful within, the more peaceful the world becomes; it all connects, like a train track.

Love conquers all

Good is stronger than bad. I believe this wholeheartedly. Love comes from goodness and has the potential to heal and nurture. Love is very much underestimated in my eyes. I feel that it can travel and spread positive energy across the globe and that if more of us allowed our natural healing love to shine, many of the negatives that are present in our world today could be eliminated.

I also believe there is more good in the world than bad, but in this multimedia world in which we now live, we are exposed to more of the negatives that surround us because they make the news headlines first, which is unfortunate. I try to focus more so on 'happy news', which helps me vibrate happiness and therefore happiness finds me wherever I go. SIMPLE.

Awakening is like the beginning on a journey of self-discovery. I now love myself for who I am. I am who I want to be. I trust that I am being guided and I try not to push unnecessarily. This empowers me to be the best me. If something is meant for me at any given time, then it will not pass me by. I trust that everything happens for a reason, even the challenging times come to enable us to shift ourselves back onto the right track.

Wisdom

As I continue on my spiritual path of self-discovery I recognise that I am observing things in a whole new way. My understanding is more in line now with great philosophers. It excites and inspires me when I reveal a new line of thought to myself.

When I discover a new quote or teaching that I can truly connect with, I feel as though my thoughts and understanding are confirmed. My personal wisdom is always increasing and I feel wealthier because of it.

For many people this awakening may come when your life dramatically changes for any reason, big or small. It tends to be through emotionally challenging occurrences that we are often drawn inside to heal and it is then, when we discover the Aladdin's cave of true love, that we find the ever so generous gift that we all have hidden in there. No longer do we need to search for the answer externally because it is internally you will find the true answer. If you haven't already found it, do yourself the biggest favour and take some time to get to know your true essence. It is the gift that will truly awaken all of your senses.

Changing lanes

I always found it strange that I was expected to know what I wanted to do with my life career-wise at such a young age. I never had an inclination for anything other than enjoying myself and that I did, to the horror of my parents and teachers. I never did anything bad but my unwillingness to learn frustrated them all, which now as a parent I totally understand. It is funny how your past can haunt you.

"Dwell not on the past. Use it to illustrate a point, then leave it behind. Nothing really matters except what you do now in this instant of time. From this moment onward you can be an entirely different person, filled with love and understanding, ready with an outstretched hand, uplifted and positive in every thought and deed." - Eileen Caddy

When I left school at the tender age of sixteen I had no idea what I wanted to do with my life. I suppose I just lived in the moment without even considering investing in my future. I always seemed to come through on top though. I worked in a factory and ended up a supervisor at the age of nineteen, then decided to move on and get an education. That was it, I had caught the learning bug. I craved learning new things, achieving goals. I took advantage of every opportunity that came my way. I was living life to its fullest (or so I thought). I was 'bettering' myself and was going to make my parents proud. I was going to show my son how successful I could be so that he would follow. 'Lead by example' and that I did as I became a special needs teacher.

> *"Time is a dressmaker specialising in alterations"* -Faith Baldwin

From there I fell in love, had more children and got married, my priorities changed and so did my ambitions. But that is all right as I have found true happiness which has allowed me to discover my true self. Sometimes we need to reach a lower point of expectation to allow us to find true happiness within. I no longer strive to prove myself, I do things because they feel right at that time and I know that it is OK to change direction as with every turn a different opportunity reveals itself.

> *"Everything happens for a reason.*
> *Every action has a reaction.*
> *Always remember that what is meant to be will always find a way to come about."*

Each of us has a different story to tell but we do have this in common: as circumstances arise throughout our lives, our reaction to those opportunities or hurdles determines the way our life progresses. However as the quote above states, it may not determine how our lives turn out as what is for us will not pass us.

> *"Sometimes it is the smallest decisions that can change your life forever."* - Keri Russell

As we get older we usually become more knowledgeable and empowered about how life functions. We know things move on, even though at times when we reach a pinnacle of tranquillity we will not want things to change. That is unfortunately beyond our control and it is harder to move on at these times. I always remember a saying that I heard during my transitioning period. 'If nothing ever changed there would be no butterflies.' This always helped me to move on, knowing that what may reveal itself has the potential of being so wonderful.

> *"Change always comes bearing gifts."*
> *– Price Pritchett*

Should we choose, we have the power to re-invent as many times as we want. Turning over a new leaf, changing our attitudes, it is all our choice. We are in the driving seat when it comes to deciding which roads to take. When I was young my mum told me, "Sometimes a change is as good as a rest". I see now that she was saying we can exhaust ourselves going down the one road, so it is sometimes good to change lanes to have a respite from the fast lane.

Things change. We should embrace these changes as they are a part of us and who we ultimately become. Some of us change more often than others. No matter how young or old we are, we still change. It is just our taste for life which is different. I like to look at life like a box of chocolates. Even though we may have indulged in all of the 'best' ones at the start of life, only leaving the unsavoury ones for later, don't just give up; because if you allow your taste to change you can enjoy the remaining flavours just as much.

So let's all embrace the changes that come our way, as they have the potential to help us all to become butterflies.

Karen Weaver

How time goes by

Time. Sometimes it flies by and at other times it goes by really slowly. On the days when time is going fast there are not enough hours in the day and on the days when time is going slowly, I can't wait for the day to end and I am in bed early. I have to admit that I am usually lacking a few hours every day. I just love life and doing different things and I never seem to have enough time to do them all. It is strange and kind of cruel how the timekeeper of life decided to make time go fast when we are happy and slow when we are not.

A quote from Harvey Mac Kay gave me food for thought:

"Time is free, but it is priceless. You can't own it, but you can use it. You can't keep it, but you can spend it. Once you've lost it you can never get it back."

Since moving to Australia my life has moved at an ever increasing pace. It is as if my foot is jammed on the accelerator and I can't reach the brake to slow things down, or maybe I don't want to reach it as I am enjoying the ride too much! But the speed of time doesn't change. Life may appear to be somewhat faster because I am enjoying it more, living within the present moment.

On a different note, the two years previous to coming here were a total contrast as time seemed to go by so slowly. Life was not happy at this time and I was in a period of waiting for things to come together and move on, so I was not enjoying the moment and time seemed to drag. This quote by Mini Zenny captures how I felt:

"When lost in depression it goes slower because you're dwelling on the past and the future. You are no longer in the present and even though you may feel you have a few extra seconds they are wasted as you are lacking in the true experience, the freedom of breathing what life offers you."

A simple daily example that I feel most mums will relate to is when I have something I want or need to do when the kids go to bed. That last hour before they finally retreat seems to drag on and on. Then whenever the time does come around for me to do the 'me thing', time goes by so quickly again. It seems so unfair but I suppose that's life.

A quote by the great thinker Albert Einstein puts time in perspective:

"The only reason for time is so that everything doesn't happen at once."

However we can slow the pace of our lives by consciously becoming more aware of how things have been rushing past, and making the decision to bring life, for a time, back to a sustainable level of nothingness. We all have the power to do this.

Some of my best, most treasured moments are when I slow down to the pace of my children. I take my 'musts' out of the picture and I go slow and sometimes silly. It is fun and quite interesting to see the world through the eyes of a child again.

We all complain that life is going by so fast but we don't seem to realise that we all have the power of time out. By choosing to take control and go slow, I discovered that I did not sacrifice my happiness, in fact I enjoyed 'quality time', which sometimes we can deprive ourselves of.

If we do take the time to organise our lives more efficiently we may discover there is more time available.

> *"For every minute spent organising, an hour is earned." www.thinkexist.com*

It's an interesting thought, maybe one worth pursuing. I don't like to be rigid when it comes to lists but I do appreciate the productivity potential when I do have a list.

One thing that

Reach for the stars

A news report that volunteers were being sought to go on a trip to mars caught my attention. There was only one problem - it was a one way ticket.

An article by Jonathan Nally states:

'Professors Dirk Schulze-Makuch and Paul Davies have suggested one-way colonisation missions to the Red Planet …"We envision that Mars exploration would begin and proceed for a long time on the basis of outbound journeys only," said Schulze-Makuch.'

I cannot comprehend the personal sacrifices that any of those who volunteer to go on this mission will be making but they must really have dedicated themselves to their jobs to even consider it as an option. Some people work so hard focusing on one ultimate goal in life that sometimes they can miss out on normal everyday things. By deciding to experience the one thing that means the most to them they are not experiencing all that life has to offer. That's all right but what keeps coming into my mind is this: What if they got to Mars and decided they had changed their minds? What if they suddenly realised they had achieved their goal and then decided they wanted to try something else? To me this offer of achieving this type of life-time goal comes at too high a cost. It also highlights how different we all are. We are all individual and we all have individual goals that we want to achieve in our life.

"Keep steadily before you the fact that all true success depends at last upon yourself." Theodore T. Hunger

I am a true believer that anyone can be whatever they want to be and that they can have whatever they want to have, they only have to want it enough. Not everyone thinks big, which is a good thing as there would be nobody to do the smaller jobs which are just as important and they keep society ticking along at a steady pace. My favourite paid job was working in a food deli. It was hard work cooking and serving customers all day but I loved it. I was also completing a college course to enable me to 'better myself' and at that time in my life I valued success in terms of the job I could get, how many exams I could pass and how much money I could earn.

I have since discovered that success for me in life is not based on how much I earn or how big a job I get. Success for me is being happy. I have worked hard to be happy and I can honestly say that I am.

"There is only one success -- to be able to spend your life in your own way." Christopher Morley

Happiness for me is raising my children and writing when I can. I feel so fortunate to have discovered my passion for writing. This did come after I experienced a very low point in my life but once I shook myself off and started to climb out of the big hole that exploded beneath me, the only way was up.

I recently had the urge to reach for the stars myself as an opportunity arose that I could not resist, even though I had just had baby number four a few weeks earlier. I took on the challenge to write a fifty thousand word novel during the month of November. I did it. I don't know how, but I did it. I felt inspired by something Whoopi Goldberg said one day on her show and it blossomed in my head from there. I took it day by day and tried my best to keep up with my daily word count and it just came together. Writing a book was a goal for me throughout my life and I achieved it and it did not affect my time with my children, which I was not willing to sacrifice. It was only the ironing and a few hours less sleep that were affected, but that was the sacrifice I made for my goal and it was worth it.

"Success is the sum of small efforts, repeated day in and day out." Robert Collier

I share this because I feel that 'where there is a will there is a way'. If you really want to do something the only person stopping you is you.

Shakespeare also had the right idea when he said:

"To climb steep hills requires a slow pace at first."

Depending on circumstances we experience at certain times during our existence our goals may change, and that's all right. We are only human and we are allowed to change our minds. We can all reach for the stars in our own way, doing what means the most to us at that time in our lives and it doesn't have to be as extreme as going to Mars!

Our universal minds

It has become more widely recognised that 'Our thoughts create things'. Those of us who open ourselves up to the possibility of being more than just one physical being in one lifetime are becoming more of a universal thinker. It may seem out of this world initially but when you open yourself to the possibilities you will soon discover that it is easier than you first perceived. In fact, it soon will become second nature.

Energy

Everything in the world is energy because we all derive from atoms which are ENERGY! At the beginning of the evolution of everything that exists you can be sure it began as an atom. As humans we are affected by the energies that surround us. The energies we release can be picked up on, especially the frequency of others if they are tuned into us through emotional connection.

A few days ago I had a very unsettling feeling and couldn't shift it no matter how hard I tried. My kids picked up on it and they were more cranky than usual and anything I did just didn't work, my computer wouldn't even switch on. I went to work that evening and I could feel myself pulsating like a beacon. I ensured that my external demeanor did not portray my inner feelings yet still my friend came to me and asked if I was OK as she felt very uneasy for me. When I got home and checked my messages, I had messages from close friends and relatives near and far asking if I was OK. They had all tapped into and picked up on my energy like energy hackers. This is just one little tiny example of the greatness that is the universal communication network, no wires required.

It can be quite an overwhelming thing to realise that through our thoughts and feelings we create our own future through the Law of Attraction. We don't need to feel like that, we just need to understand it for the simplicity that it is. As I understand it, the more things I do to make me happy, the more things come my way to make me happy. I remember once doing a personal development activity in which I had to write down twenty sentences beginning with 'I WANT'. Then one by one I had to delete them from that list until I only had one left. I found it hard to pick between the last two as one was about the happiness of my son and the other, which I did pick, stated:

"I want to always be happy, because when I am happy those who love me are happy too."

The lady who facilitated the group was overwhelmed when she read it.

So many of us seek externally for happiness. Many people search in this way for a lifetime but it is those of us who realise that true happiness comes from connecting within who live a fulfilled life. All of the answers we need to guide us through our life reside within. When we listen to our inner spirit guide we cannot fail because it is then wisdom finds us; wisdom that we never knew we had begins to shine through.

We are all sent messages from the Universe that we can pick up when we open our internal receptors. We put out our requests for what we want our life experience to be and the Genie of the Universe will show us the way to achieve our heart's desires. All we have to do is be aware of the signs. These messages may come through conversations with others, a serendipitous encounter or you may simply be drawn towards something that will lead you to your goal or you may have a moment of inspiration. Whatever way you are guided, it all starts with you being aware of the signs the Universe sends your way.

We will however receive these messages clearer and stronger when we stand still; this may be through meditating, resting or praying, whichever way works for us at the time.

Avoiding unfortunate events

Since becoming more aware I know that I have avoided many unfortunate occurrences. The only way I can describe this is that a signal will be sent to me in the form of a warning. For example, if I am rushing about and everything seems to be going against me, it is for a reason. I no longer stress about it because it is happening for a reason. Maybe that red traffic light is preventing me from having an accident or maybe by the kids not wanting to go somewhere it is stopping me from having an unwanted encounter. All I know is that since I have begun reacting to the universal signs that guide me I have had a less stressful journey through life.

When you are going against that grain and travelling down the wrong path in life, the universe will let you know. When everything is going against us it is worthwhile reflecting on past events. Should we keep pushing forward because anything worth having is hard fought? For me, I would take on board lessons learned and wait for the way to be revealed. Life is the adventure that we want it to be and the universe will help us live it the way we want to should we so choose.

Opening ourselves to receiving.

There are so many people who are not open to receiving. They give so much but don't feel worthy enough to receive the gifts they so rightly deserve. We first have to want something in order for it to manifest into reality. It is not for us to determine HOW we will reach our destination that is the domain of the universe; it is however, our duty to clearly request what we want to experience in life. When we have done this then it is up to us to open ourselves to receiving and act on the signs sent to us. It is a simple process that can often be mistaken for something far more complicated.

Challenge this today. Clearly request something you want. Shout it out loud, write it down or tell someone else. Then feel what it is like to have it, close your eyes and believe that you have it. Keep the faith that the universe will deliver by express courier exactly what you want, it IS on its way. Act on opportunity when it comes to you. At least once a day take a moment to feel what it is like to have it, get excited, smile from ear to ear, and jump up and down. Why? Well because by feeling it, it will bring it to you quicker.

Gratitude

Definition of gratitude: "The quality of being thankful; readiness to show appreciation for and to return kindness."

Appreciation for what one has already accomplished is a valuable trait to possess as it will keep you balanced. Being grateful is not rated highly enough by most people nor is it used to a level of fulfilment for many. Most of us focus on the things we want to achieve, the things we want; we crave more to fill a void, a need for more. It is all fine and well to set personal goals and work towards them but in order to have a happy balance we must not forget to express gratitude for what we have already.

Children know fully the benefits of gratitude as they discover the joys of living each and every day to its full potential. One of the first things most of us are taught when we are young is to say thank you. I know that gratitude is one of the main morals I ensure my children learn in the hope they will value everything they receive. I do find it strange how so many people decide to disregard this wonderful trait as they get older. If only they knew they are also disregarding the opportunity to effortlessly attract more things to be grateful for into their lives.

If someone is truly grateful for something you have done for them then you wouldn't mind doing something again, would you? I believe the universe works that way too. If we are full of appreciation for what we receive, we automatically send out a signal of gratitude that will attract more for us to be grateful for.

Give to receive and receive to give

In this life there are 'givers' and there are 'takers'. An interesting observation I have made is that the 'givers' find it very hard to receive in return, as they get their rewards from the feeling of giving and so are fulfilled in the giving. The 'takers' have learned that in order to fulfil their desire of receiving they must learn to give also. In order to have the wonderful feeling that giving is, we need to be able to receive also.

Top ten reasons to be grateful

1. It increases your satisfaction with life.
2. It reduces the damaging feelings of envy and resentment and instead creates feelings of happiness and joy.
3. You will recover faster and more successfully from negative events.
4. You will possess higher levels of vitality and optimism.
5. People who are grateful have less stress.
6. You will attract more things to be grateful about.
7. Being grateful lets you enjoy the simple but good things in life.

8. Being grateful allows you to take power from negatives and focus more on positives.

9. It refocuses your priorities to what is fundamentally important to you.

10. It improves your physical and emotional well-being.

There are many people who practise gratitude daily, reporting that their lives have improved. As we practise gratitude, something very powerful happens; instead of being happy and then depressed, then happy again as if on an emotional rollercoaster, we become grateful, which creates balance. This balance means we are easier to please and we will feel more of a sense of calm and peace. It is through consistent practice that we become more aware that we are simply part of a greater power as we expand our awareness.

Ten examples of gratefulness

1. I am grateful for being alive and having a healthy and prosperous life.

2. I am so grateful that my children are perfect in mind, body and spirit, that they are awake and aware of our evolutionary time.

3. I am so grateful that in my whole life I have attracted fantastic friends who have helped along the way.

4. I am grateful for my family, all my friends and loving people.

5. I am grateful for all that has happened until now and all that I am consciously creating from now on.

6. I am grateful for nature's splendour.

7. I am grateful for the fresh, clean, free air which fills my lungs full of life every moment.

8. I am grateful for the sun, moon and stars that create wonderful energy.

9. I am grateful for adopt a mum.

10. I am grateful for gratitude and the abundance of things I can be grateful for.

Why not invest in a 'Gratitude corkboard'? Write down the things you are personally grateful for on pieces of paper and stick them to it, constantly adding to it as you progress through life. This will always remind you to be grateful for what matters to you whenever you see it.

When we express gratitude often, we allow out heart centre to open up. By doing so we are allowing ourselves to be connected with other people; so ultimately it gives us the power to love and be loved. By being aware of how being grateful can help us connect more deeply with ourselves, we can become more noble.

"As we express our gratitude, we must never forget that the highest appreciation is not to utter words, but to live by them." John F.Kennedy

We need to also show appreciation to others for the things they have done for us by putting into action our gratitude. Many people do this by sending flowers, cards or something that is personal to the 'giver' in order to show sincere appreciation. But thanking someone does not have to be expensive or we would end up wishing that others would not help us. We can show others appreciation in our actions; a hug or kiss with a simple acknowledgement is enough reward for many. How about sending them some positive energy the next time you have a moment of thought? We can never have enough positive energy coming our way.

So let's promise ourselves that from now on we will take a quiet moment to be grateful for all we have already received. By doing so, we release a negative and replace it with a positive.

Choices and values, past or present?

I was reading an interview with January Jones in the West Weekend magazine about her role in *Mad Men*, a television series set in 1960s New Orleans. She commented, "It's a nostalgia that even I feel. Women have so many choices now but I think maybe the world was a nicer place then – happier and simpler." This struck a chord with me. I do value the rights and choices I have as a woman in the 21st century but I can't help thinking that in earlier years values were more family focused and the sense of community was stronger. Crime also was prominent in my thoughts as I believe there was more value on human life then and criminal elements were not as widespread as they are today.

On the topic of family life, there was more value on a marriage and it was not something entered into on a whim because it was for life. Women stuck at their marriages knowing that it was hard work to maintain them with housework and children keeping them busy from dawn to dusk and little time for much else. This was bound to put strains on relationships but with the sense of community and most families in the same situation there was a sense of just getting on with the tasks in hand. The multi-tasking abilities of most women mainly benefited their husbands and children. Although I believe many husbands took advantage of their wives in many ways by abusing their trust and taking what they did for granted during these times because they did not value them as an equal in the relationship. Life was also harder as technology was not as advanced and globalisation had not yet fully impacted on societies. Women had it tough then but are we getting it tougher these days as society puts more and more pressure on us to be super human. The safety of children was not as prominent then. Children were allowed a lot more freedom and had more of a sense of adventure. There was not the need to keep such to be such a close eye on them then either, but does that mean there was not the same level of? Back then people trusted each other more but was that a good thing? Did that make children more vulnerable then or now?

I could debate pros and cons all day in my head and feel that I am running around trying to catch my tail with no hope of reaching a conclusion on the subject but I do know this. Back then there were still choices for women just not as many. This could be a good thing for those who find problems with making decisions and who may in this day and age feel pressures from society and that they are under achieving. For others who are ambitious and who may have felt trapped by boundaries in western society in the past, the world is now their oyster as there are no boundaries except those implemented through law. Time moves on and things change but who dictates the pace? The world is moving at such a fast pace now that anyone can be forgiven for not keeping up.

What kind of world are the children of today going to be rearing their children in? Maybe some of the values of old will make a comeback in the same way as do great fashion statements of the past. I can only hope there is opportunity for true happiness in every element of life.

Wisdom

"To acquire knowledge, one must study; but to acquire wisdom one must observe." Marilyn Von Savant

I respect wisdom whole-heartedly. I appreciate that it does tend to come with age but I also feel it comes when we open our hearts and minds to a wider spectrum of being.

Definition of Wisdom: *"Wisdom is a deep understanding and realizing of people, things, events or situations, resulting in the ability to choose or act or inspire to consistently produce the optimum results with a minimum of time, energy or thought."* Wikipedia

Great Thinkers

Many great thinkers past and present have expressed themselves generously. When we are willing to really listen and search beyond their words to the meaning behind them, we can access their wisdom as they visit deeper realms of reality, introducing us to an even deeper reasoning. This is more fulfilling than the everyday thought processes many of us have accustomed ourselves to. They convey a gift of alternative thoughts which when opened can bring magic into the lives of those willing to receive.

Albert Einstein, Sir Isaac Newton, William Shakespeare, Pablo Picasso, Mother Theresa, Marie Curie, Leonardo Da Vinci, Aristotle, Sigmund Freud, Charles Darwin and most recently Louise Hay, Oprah Winfrey and so many more beautiful souls have used their creative means to spread the knowledge they have within to help others.

"Follow your instincts. That's where true wisdom manifests itself."- Oprah Winfrey

I believe true wisdom finds us when we open ourselves up and let it in. Wisdom comes from knowing what it is that truly makes us happy and doing it well to the best of our natural ability. The secret to living a fulfilling life is to be happy; it is the way something makes us feel that triggers us to prioritise events as they have occurred.

I believe wise people are always open to learning more and are willing to share their acquired knowledge with others in the bid to help them reach a greater understanding for themselves. Life is quite simple but many people like to make it complicated. Everything in life that we do…work, socialise, sleep, eat, exercise, have children… everything we choose to do has a direct connection to the pursuit of happiness. Just think about it, how many things do you do to create happiness for yourself or others?

I feel fortunate that I have reached a wonderful level of personal wisdom. I know what makes me happy and I am aware of all of the energies around me. I live a happy and fulfilled life doing exactly what I know works for me. It may not be someone else's cup of tea, but if we all were happy doing the same things the world would be a very boring place. Also through my writing I have the opportunity to share with others my thoughts as I grow in knowledge and wisdom. I look forward to always becoming wiser every day as more and more of life reveals itself to me. One thing I have come to realise which I find beneficial is that wisdom often requires control of my emotions and passions; this will make way for my principles, reasoning and accumulated knowledge to prevail and determine my actions.

"By three methods we may learn wisdom: First, by reflection, which is noblest; second, by imitation, which is easiest; and third by experience, which is the bitterest." Confucius

Books of knowledge

"Honesty is the first chapter of the book of wisdom." Abraham Lincoln

Books are a wonderful source of accessing wisdom from others. There are many timeless books through the ages that continue to pass on knowledge and wisdom through the generations. Books are the vehicle through which great thinkers – from the past and in the present – can reach many people in moments of intimacy and learning.

One such timeless book is *The Book of Wisdom*, formerly known as Book of the Wisdom of Solomon. This is a book of the Bible and one of seven wisdom books of the Old Testament. It has been used as a reference for many a great thinker.

However, even though books are a great source for seeking wisdom and we may relate and attain guidance from many wonderful books, I believe true wisdom can only be obtained through experience, self-awareness, conflict, forgiveness, peace and realisation on our own personal journey. This can come with age and/or conscious awareness.

Have you ever wondered about the saying, 'A wise old owl'? It is because an owl sits and waits, taking in all that is happening around him and turning his head full circle as only he can, being aware and acting only when it is necessary. Are there any other characteristics you can think of as to why an owl is deemed to be wise and could you possibly apply these attributes to yourself?

Inspiration

Definition of Inspiration: The process of being mentally stimulated to do or feel something, esp. to do something creative: "flashes of inspiration". freedictionary.com

As a writer the best thing ever is the feeling of inspiration. That light-bulb moment is like a gift from the universe and for me it conjures up emotions of excitement and passion. These inspirational moments enable me to express my innermost thoughts. It is also a way for me to use my imagination and convey it creatively through writing.

Creative self-expression is different for everyone. Some people like to paint to articulate their creative impulses, others may choose pottery, photography, design or dance. There are so many ways of releasing the wonderment that is creative impulses. The opportunity for self-expression is something I will always ensure that my children have close to them at all times.

When we allow ourselves to "BE" our awareness is at a heightened level. We are absorbing things we would not normally see whilst rushing around doing our everyday things. Through this state of awareness inspirational influences can be heightened and we may feel the desire to express and share these findings with others.

However sometimes inspiration doesn't find us and we may need to find it. In his article "Eight Methods to find inspiration," Mike King shares some tips on how to do this.

1. Search out new experiences – Inspiration is heightened when exposing ourselves to new experiences. By visiting new places, people or environments you may feel inspired. The potential to educate or express your perception of these new changes in your state of awareness may instigate a passion to do so in whatever form of creative self- expression you choose. We are all inspired differently and that's what makes the world so interesting.

2. Keep an open mind – By being open minded you will fight back any fear or doubt linked to your inspirational impulse. As a writer I could limit myself because of my own inhibitions or the possible negative perceptions of others. Choosing to embrace the inspiration and explore and share can only lead to feeling wonderfully fulfilled.

3. Watch your emotions – Keep emotions in check, try to not allow them to blind you from seeing what you dare to see or what you dare to believe. An example of this is fear of how others perceive your work. Others may not see things as you envision them but try not to let fear stop you from exploring. Emotions can also be good as they can be signals directing you towards finding inspiration that you feel connected to which can only increase the joyous feeling that being inspired brings.

4. Share the Experience – Talking about what you experience with others makes inspiration become real and it also has the potential to grow quite quickly. An initial snowflake of inspiration may snowball down the slope of another's inspiring offerings. This is when magic can happen. Beautiful bonds can develop from connections like this.

5. Seek out solitude – On the other hand, stillness can offer you a way to connect with your mind, body and surroundings. By allowing your mind to wander at this time, with focus and consciousness your initial inspiration can spiral out to a magnificent creation. Some people do not enjoy such times of solitude. As a writer I value them highly as it is during these times of complete solitude that I can release all of the information I have stored and put it in order. Others, however, may use this time to connect spiritually in prayer, meditation or for personal enhancement through study or deep thought. All of these assist in calming the emotions, alert the senses and create more awareness and will guide you towards further opportunities for inspiration.

6. Keep in mind your role models – Do you have one? If so keep in mind whatever it is about them that inspires you and use that inspiration to seek out more. Does your role model steer you in a direction you are passionate about? Check that you are seeking inspiration in the areas of life that provide you with heartfelt

inspiration or is it your role model steering you more towards social influences? It is worth remembering that we can change our role models as we change in our lives, reflecting what is important to you in the now.

7. Align your actions – Instigating action with our inspirations reinforces them in our minds which quickly builds a neural connection in the brain with both the action and the inspiration. It thus strengthens the connection and may drive a desire to learn more. Taking action on new inspirations will strengthen them and their associations to other inspirations which will lead to developing new beliefs and passions.

8. Follow your faith – Sometimes inspiration does not come easily but if you learn to trust in your own judgment towards knowing what matters, no matter what the source your intuition will guide you. Having faith in this guidance, whether or not you deem it to be spiritual, may mean the difference between finding inspiration and not finding it.

Please note that the comments accompanying each tip are my own.

Being more aware of our surroundings by adjusting our eyes to take in a more peripheral angle rather than just the restrictions of tunnel vision allows us to see the bigger picture. This assists us to be exposed to more and more opportunities to be inspired.

Awareness is a key that unlocks my inspiration. Also, taking a step back and thinking outside the box can give me an alternative perspective to my thoughts, guiding me on a new trail of thought that I may not otherwise have ventured down. It comes back to having an open mind, not a closed, judgmental one.

I find being aware of how people act in different environments really inspiring and it always gives me food for thought. When out and about at your local shop or centre, try to give yourself a few moments to sit and be aware of all of your surroundings. You will see things you didn't see before and it can truly be inspiring.

Why not start your own inspiration board to remind you of the beautiful things in life that inspire you?

Maybe a raindrop falling from a leaf, or the next time the sun rises and beams a fireball of light that cascades over every treetop and sweeps across the landscape. This type of natural beauty can truly be inspiring. It may provide you with a smile or an idea to write a book, paint a picture, sculpt a work of art, write a poem or take a picture to capture its essence. Whatever approach we may take to capture that moment and make it our very own is an inspiration in itself.

My thought for my inspiration board: *Life is filled with magnificent beauty if only we adjust our eyes to see it, then we reveal its true splendor.*

Karen Weaver

I'm a believer

Definition of Belief: *"Mental acceptance of a claim as truth; something believed; The quality or state of believing. Something one accepts as true or real; a firmly held opinion or conviction."* www.wiktionary.org

The Beatles believed so much they sang the song *I'm a Believer* about it and look what success it brought them.

"I thought love was only true in fairy tales; Meant for someone else but not for me. Oh, love was out to get me;
That's the way it seems. Disappointment haunted all my dreams."

When I look more closely at the words in the lyrics I can see a message.

"I thought love was only true in fairytales" – This shows they didn't believe it existed in reality.

"Meant for someone else but not for me" – They never believed it was possible for them.

"Oh, love was out to get me; That's the way it seems." – What is for you won't pass you.

"Disappointment haunted all my dreams" – They never believed anything other than being disappointed.

The song goes on to say, *"Then I saw her face, now I'm a believer"* so after being a non-believer and receiving nothing but disappointments, when he did start to believe all his dreams came true. This is a wonderful example of belief at its finest. If you think negatives you receive negatives, if you think positives you receive positives. Like attracts like – The laws of the universe. Believe and you shall receive.

Self-belief

One of the most important beliefs of all is self-belief. Without this we may not have the ability to function at our full potential in life. If you believe in your own capabilities then you will have the confidence to approach everyday challenges knowing you are making the right decisions for yourself and the good of others.

For someone with low self-esteem, believing in you is a very tough step to make. To increase your self-esteem in this instance experts suggested finding a mentor. Don't be afraid to ask someone to guide you; in fact you may even discover they would be flattered to help. A lot of people enjoy being given the opportunity to give as it makes them feel good, so by helping they are also gaining from the process. A win-win situation!

That 'Knowing' feeling

With belief comes an unwavering faith that something is certain and therefore it can create a feeling of Knowing. This feeling is like no other and I can only describe my experience of it as a sensation of unwavering belief that something truly wonderful is on its way. I do not know nor understand fully this feeling. All I know is that I have discovered I am not the only person who has experienced such a feeling. I have recognised that this has occurred along the way of my personal spiritual journey and after I discovered the wonderfulness of self-love.

"Knowing to me is the spirit speaking. It is not based on thoughts, it is just a sense of 'rightness' and

'knowing' about the right action or path for us. It is also in our and those close to us best interests. It is not logical, it is an intuitive sense, I believe based on the guiding 'knowings' of the spirit." Rhonda

I have studyied 'knowings' further but my discovery so far shows that this sensation is connected to our spiritual self. When we connect to this pure element of our very being we experience this belief in trusting that all will be well. A wonderful feeling indeed.

What do you believe?

We all believe in different things and this makes us all unique and keeps life interesting. Our beliefs can change over time. As we age our values can change dramatically and we grow into our true selves more influenced by our own thoughts and experiences than guided by others.

My beliefs have evolved with me throughout my journey of life thus far. I expect they will continue to evolve, but that the core belief will always be maintained, just deeper meaning and more of an understanding created.

I believe everything happens in this life for a reason and that I need to be aware of the signs I am being sent to ensure I stay on the right path for me. If something is not going well it is a sign to reconsider my options. If I am feeling sad it means I need to change something, as being sad is a sign that something isn't quite right.

As a child our beliefs can be influenced strongly by our parents and carers, but they can also be thought up through our experiences and our imagination. When I was a child I had many innocent silly beliefs on which I now look back and think how naive I was. I thought that my hair would go straight if I didn't eat the crusts of bread, I believed in fairies and in Santa until I was told at 12.

Whatever your beliefs may have been in the past, in the now, or whatever they may be in the future, the important thing is that we do believe. Through believing with all your heart on good, beautiful things can happen. Belief is a powerful tool that we all have and that we can access any time in our toolbox of hope.

Why do we label?
"Labels belong on bottles, not people."

There is a lot of stigma attached to different groups within society. Our obsession with putting a label on everyone and everything has resulted in segregation being predominant in our communities as some people are considered differently than others. If we lived in a perfect world 'labelling' would not be a problem but that is not reality and it is easier to accept that we all label at some level or other and that people have always done so.

You may think, "Hey, I don't label!" but I beg to differ because whether we admit it or not, we all do it. Generally labelling is not damaging but it makes life structured so easier to follow. The most common method of 'labeling' people derives from a general way of perceiving members of a certain nationality, religion, ethnicity, gender, or one of the many other groups in existence.

I discovered on wikipedia that labelling originated in sociology and criminology and was developed by Howard S. Becker. Becker explained that 'labelling theory' holds that deviance is not inherent to an act, but instead focuses on the linguistic tendency of majorities to negatively label minorities or those seen as deviant from the norms. This theory was prominent in the 1960s and 1970s, when some modified versions of labelling developed.

One example of damaging labelling is when considering mental health. Many people do not understand the issues related to mental health. Not being educated on the subject creates fear and with fear often comes anger and frustration and a lack of consideration for others. My view on the issue after having worked in this sector for almost four years, is that many of us may experience mental health issues on some level at some point in our lives. It is those who do not address these issues or seek help to manage them more successfully are the ones to be feared, not the people who actually do seek help. The stigma associated with mental health is detrimental for sufferers and their loved ones and even results in some people delaying seeking help.

I am a huge fan of Beyond Blue. I have referred to that site a few times now at my need of repair. I think it's fantastic that a website like this one is so broadcasted to let sufferers know that help is out there. An expression I saw on a poster once while visiting a Mental Illness centre read 'Labels belong on bottles not people.'" A friend to the end.

Labelling is a big issue in the school environment as this is an emotionally vulnerable time for many young people and being labelled can make the whole schooling experience a very unpleasant one. It can also leave a deep emotional scar on an individual for the rest of their lives. They can believe the perceptions others have of them and find it hard to move on, even if the labelers haven't given their actions a second thought. A school yard bully may often feel compelled to maintain their macho image even into adulthood as that is the perception others had. This concept may also apply for many other school-based labels.

Many people label themselves and this can be a good or bad thing depending on how critical or positive we are. We can be our harshest critics and yet we are supposed to have our own best interests at heart. This may seem contradictory but with a little applied effort we can easily rectify the situation and change our lives.

"Our self-applied labels can bind us or free us. Compare 'I am powerless' with 'I am enthusiastic and confident'. If you must label yourself, stick to positive ones, but not to the point of becoming arrogant or acting superior." Chuck Gallozi

People label to try and understand why others are different from themselves. It is perceived to be an attempt at comprehending a complex world. Socially, labels represent a way of identifying people that is thought of by many as a form of discrimination.

The thing that gets me is that a lot of people label without being knowledgeable of enough evidence justifying a 'label'.

We as humans are complex and multidimensional. When we apply labels to each other we are limiting our potential of seeing the wider picture and we are creating a narrow view of a wider complexity. Labels can hide the true contents of an individual.

How to stop labelling

When we take the time to realise why we all label each other, we then have the knowledge to assist in the process of eliminating this habit. Chuck Gallozzi suggests we can overcome labelling by cultivating unconditional acceptance, compassion and understanding and that we can learn to observe and experience the world without judgment. We can also help by remaining detached from expectations and demands that we instinctively apply at times. In doing this we learn to accept what is and people as they are. Once we understand fully the power of our words, we may decide to do more than just avoid using words, we may change to using them to encourage and inspire others instead. What a beautiful thing that would be!

A woman's touch

As women we benefit from the connections we build with the other women in our lives. Healthy relationships with a positive female influence can give us strength and knowledge beyond our imaginings. Yes, some of the women we must interact with we have not chosen but we can choose how they impact on us as women. We have the power to take negatives from those relationships and turn them into positives if we so wish.

Many of us fall in love and have children, which can distract us from our needs as women. Even though we are surrounded by our loved ones we may still feel alone inside and a simple conversation with a female friend or relative can help. Something as simple as having a cuppa, a telephone call or a conversation on a social site for women can assist in breaking down the barriers of loneliness by providing a vital link with female companionship. This can also benefit daughters who witness healthy female relationships between women as they grow up.

The loss of a close female influence such as a grandmother, mother or sister through death or other circumstances can leave a big gap which can be hard to heal. However we can help alleviate this loss by surrounding ourselves with positive female company which can only bring 'the woman's touch' back into our lives in a positive way.

The moment

I used to travel through life not thinking or caring about what other people thought of me or how they judged me. It was a kind of rebellious ideology. Since I have become more aware of me as a person and since I have become a mum, I have also become more aware of how others perceive me in the moment they encounter my presence. Maybe this is because I judge myself a little more now that I do not only have me to think about. I am more aware of the thoughts and reactions of others

I must stress that not all judgments are bad. I was travelling on a bus to our local beach one day and my two children were both having separate conversations with me which went on for a while. A man complimented me on how I could have two conversations going at once and how well I interacted with them both. On this occasion I never even thought about how I was being perceived (I was too busy having two conversations), but I have to admit it was so nice of the man to say that as most people would not have said anything.

A stark contrast to this is when one or more of my children are playing up in public. It is quite embarrassing and I am sure in that moment many people are judging my children's behaviour. However my initial reaction is to defuse the situation and deal with the issue they are obviously having. There have been occasions when I have overheard comments like, "She would need to put manners on those children" and other horrid judgmental comments. I must stress that I do not allow the judgments of others influence my parenting choices, nor do I allow such comments to affect me personally. I am just more aware of them, especially when they are expressed purely with the intention of me hearing them.

This has made me more aware of my reactions and reflects on how I interact with others. I am forever putting my foot in it by saying things just for the sake of saying things at times. I think I am doing well at the time but when I reflect on some conversations I end up wishing I had thought before I spoke. I can give the impression of being scatty when I am actually well educated. I suppose that this is why I like to write. I can think about what I am going to write before I write it and I can always hit the delete button. When the moment of conversation has passed I have often wished I could hit the delete button but of course in the reality of life that is not possible.

I have come to realise that although it is good to be aware of what is going on around me, I have no control over others' thoughts and I should not try to as we are all individuals with our own traits. If others judge me in the moment they encounter me, well so be it. I have no control over their perceptions of me but I do have the power over my perceptions of me and that is what matters

How we adjust

Definition of adjustment: *"The act of adjusting; adaptation to a particular condition, position, or purpose."* freedictionary.com.

I am always amazed at how we as humans can adjust to our surroundings. As things change around us we incrementally adjust, sometimes without us even noticing. Consistently changing global influences and personal changes all contribute to continuous adjustments in our lives. Think about it! Do you do anything differently now than when you were a child?

I watched a programme that highlighted how climate change is affecting Senegal. The masses of people coming from the country to the capital, Dakar, is of such a magnitude that the city is not able to cope. This country is the most affected by climate change in the whole world. Their rivers are swelling and consuming the land. I was fascinated to hear how in these areas they have changed from eating chickens to eating ducks because ducks float. Also they are now growing vegetables and other food sources on their roofs.

We all may end up having to adjust and learn new survival techniques, maybe even resorting to providing for ourselves and being more self-sufficient – and if not us, then our children or our children's children. How do we prepare for this adjustment? Are we moving backwards? Only time will tell. But what I do know is that the human race is adaptable and you may have heard the saying, "What doesn't kill us only makes us stronger."

Physical adjustment

When our physical surroundings change, we adjust. This may be because we have chosen 'a change of scenery'. For example, if we go on holidays, move house or country or if we decide to experience something different such as a new sport. The possibilities are endless. It may also be due to an exterior influence such as a natural disaster, or we have been forced to go somewhere, or simply the weather changes things. These are all physical adjustments we may experience in our lifetime.

Emotional adjustment

Internal adjustment can be a more challenging experience. The shift from what is familiar to what is unknown or unwanted may be fearful but if we allow the process of transition to occur by dealing with emotions as they present themselves, it will be an easier adjustment. Emotional adjustments may include falling in love, having a baby, losing a loved one or experiencing something that challenges your morals.

"Happiness comes from... some curious adjustment to life." Hugh Walpole

When people who are not enjoying life take the time to adjust their thoughts to a more positive perspective they may experience the delightful magic that is life. This gift to themselves can be one of the most transformational adjustments that will ever occur in their lives. This is a powerful adjustment and those who choose to be aware of their thoughts will be stronger, no matter what scenario may face them in the future.

When I moved to Australia in 2008 from Ireland, not only was there the drastic contrasting climate for my body to adjust to quite quickly, there was also a different culture to embrace. Although we all talked the same language there are many words and sayings unique to Australia that we had to learn. I was open to this adjustment and so by embracing this wonderful gift I have flourished in this new setting.

For many of us becoming a mum is one of the biggest adjustments we make in our life. When a baby comes into someone's life it can turn things upside down. Some people deal with it better than others but no matter what the circumstances, all mums will experience an adjustment on some level. I am aware that for the rest of my life I am connected to my children, no matter what path they may take. I am always adjusting as they grow and learning as I go along, because they are all unique. I feel fortunate that I am open to this adjustment.

There are millions of scenarios of adjustment affecting people every day and yet we survive because 'we get on with it'. What may not be a big adjustment for me may be a very big adjustment to someone else.

There are really great things occurring that bring wonderful adjustments, but not all adjustments are this positive. Having a happier perception of the inevitable changes that come our way is like waving a magic wand at those experiences, adjusting them to suit your life – not you adjusting to accommodate them.

One thing is for sure, things are going to keep changing

and we are going to keep adjusting. If we approach these changes with an open, positive outlook we will live happily. If we try to control or influence these changes we may get frustrated or anxious that we are unable to control our lives successfully. We may have to or decide to change the plans we have for our life. By being open to such adjustments we are choosing a smoother journey. So why not just go with the flow and see where life brings you!

Life is beautiful!

Friendship

Definition of friendship: "The state of being friends; friendly relation, or attachment, to a person, or between persons; affection arising from mutual esteem and good will; friendliness; amity; good will." Brainyquote.com

Friendship is not something that immediately happens. It takes time to build a strong bond with someone else. Some people do 'click' on their initial meeting but largely friendships occur because of circumstances in our lives during certain times.

Friendships can happen anywhere whenever we are open to them entering our lives. I believe we need to have a space where they can enter, like a vacant position, because a friendship, whether it is a general acquaintance or a lifelong bond, still requires a certain amount of positive energy to maintain it. That fact must be identified and appreciated by each party.

Friendship is a gift, one of the greatest gifts we can share with another. Friendships are so special that they take root in our hearts. So that is why we all deserve the best when it comes to who we share this precious gift with. Only lucky people are said to have 'true friends'.

We all have our own different ideals of what we want from friendships. There is a big difference in what a man wants from his friendships and what a woman wants from hers. Some friendships start out good and then may turn sour. It is advised not to hang on to these relationships as they can be emotionally damaging. However, when a friendship has a positive effect on our life, magical things can happen.

Different types of friendships.

There are many different types of friendships. We will all probably end up in some category at one time or another to different people and we may make friends in each category at different stages of our lives. These friends may display different qualities to us. Friendships can range from complex to simple.

- Associates - People with whom we share a common activity, such as a hobby or sport.
- Useful contacts - People who share information and advice with us, typically related to work or advancing one's career.
- Favour friends - People who help each other out in a functional manner, but not in an emotional manner.
- Fun friends - People who socialise together, but only for fun. Not committing to providing each other with a deep level of emotional support.
- Helpmates - A combination of favour friends and fun friends. Socialising together and also helping each other out in a functional manner.
- Comforters - Like helpmates, but they also provide emotional support.
- Confidants – Someone we disclose personal information to and who we enjoy spending time with, but aren't always in a position to offer practical help, for example if they live far away.

- Soulmates - Have all of the elements.

Qualities of a friend

What qualities do you look for in a friend? Qualities that you respect or may want for yourself? Someone to whom you are similar? Does it matter? Have you ever thought about what type of friend you attract? True friends usually possess numerous qualities and that is why they are treasured so much. A friend may have some qualities and you may have others, therefore complementing each other.

- Loyalty – stick with you no matter what.
- Humour - A friend to laugh with who makes you feel good.
- Sensitivity – An ideal quality to have a sensitive side. Compassion and understanding.
- Intelligence – Someone of similar intelligence to you can make friendships easier.
- Good company – We need friends that we enjoy spending time with or what is the point?
- Listener – A strong quality; sometimes we all need time to pour our heart out, especially at difficult times.
- Common sense – Friends are often people we trust to guide us; we need them to know what they are talking about.
- Trustworthy – You should be able to trust your friend no matter what. A key quality.
- Generosity – Good friends are giving of their time, love and knowledge; a generous spirit.
- Honesty- A friend should be honest, tell you what you need to hear, not what you want to hear.

Not every friend has ALL of these qualities. It is a tough list to meet. Good friends may have many of them, but you may discover that your soulmate/best friend will be the person in your life who has all or most of these qualities.

Friendship is something which is hard to describe. The word 'friend' too can mean different things to different people. But the main thing which is known to all is that a friend is someone who will offer a shoulder to cry on, encourage and guide as and when required."

These bonds don't just happen, they grow. I like to think of the process like this: When we are born we are all given a bag of magic friendship seeds and we must find perfect plots to plant these seeds in. The seeds may flourish in some areas really beautifully, more productively in many and not take at all to others. When the seed and the plot work together amazing things happen and true friendships blossom.

"A friend will strengthen you with her prayers, bless you with her love, and encourage you with her hope."

I have had many friendships throughout my life. I cherish each of them for different reasons. Many have provided me with treasured memories. I am fortunate enough to say that most have had a positive impact on my life in some way. Some have stood the test of time and I still have contact but others have sort of fizzled out as our lives went in different directions. Life is full of changes and this sometimes includes friendships.

I am so fortunate to have a strong friendship bond with my sister which I feel is a wonderful connection. It was strained for some time but it has stood the test of time because of forgiveness and love, and I am grateful for this.

I have also found true friendship which I value so deeply through adopt-a-mum, I have to admit that I did not expect to have meaningful bonds through an internet site but I have surprisingly discovered that I can be my true self and I don't worry about how I look or how I am perceived. I just get to be me. This I can only be described as sheer freedom. To think that I held myself back when I could touch so many people in a positive way. This fills me with so much joy and I treasure the beautiful bonds as true friendships.

This is a small insight to my friendship garden. Lots of seeds planted at the beginning but only so many blossoming. The laws of the friendship garden are that the most cared for flowers blossom beautifully and every now and again new exciting seedlings full of love blossom. Why not take a moment to reflect on how your 'Friendship Garden' has grown?

Can you keep a secret?

Can you keep a secret? Many people will answer 'Yes'. But let me ask that question a different way. Do you want to keep a secret? Some people will answer 'Yes' but I will answer 'No'. Secrets are part of our lives whether we like it or not; everyone has them in some shape or form. Small or big, intentional or protective, they for the most part contain deceit and almost certainly someone is in the process of getting hurt. In many instances there can be no good that comes from a secret and it can manifest into something bigger the longer it goes on.

Secret. Take a moment to think of the word. Things that may come to mind initially could be, not open or public, mysterious, hidden, designed to exclude detection, not expressed or confidential.

I grew up thinking it wonderful and special that someone would want to share a secret with me. I was so excited by the mystery of it all. As I have grown older I'm more in the understanding that things are better kept open for all to see. Why hide things? Why not deal with them and move on?

Why do we feel the need to keep secrets?

Keeping information about us to ourselves serves a purpose in that it can help people feel independent and unique. It actually starts as a natural, instinctive process when we are children and is an important step in a child's independent growth.

When we are adults we may feel the need to avoid negative judgments from others and therein lies the reason behind many a secret. This can be potentially dangerous because the fear of revelation can mean that a secret digs deeper roots.

Secrets can come to us in different ways. They may be personal secrets that we keep hidden within ourselves and choose not to share, maybe out of good intentions not to hurt someone's feelings. These types of secrets can lie dormant at the back of our minds but they will need to be addressed at some point.

There are, however, generally secretive people and it definitely does not mean they are bad, it just indicates that they are private in the way they conduct their personal lives and they should not be judged because of that.

Many families hold secrets, probably because of family loyalty, to save embarrassment or even to protect someone within the family. These types of secrets if held throughout the years have the potential to manifest into bigger issues, because people may go to great lengths to ensure their secret is not revealed.

Many people who have researched the history of their family will discover secrets, usually kept because the issue was perceived to be unacceptable socially at that time. Have you ever thought about the outcasts or rebels within a family? Think about it - are they the people who are open and honest with everyone and not willing to be sucked into the world of secrecy?

Also think about it. If someone in your family was seriously ill and hid that from you to spare you the worry, would you feel that that they intentionally deceived you?

Some people have a secret life. They go to great lengths to portray a certain lifestyle to those they know and love but in the background they are doing something secretly that they do not acknowledge to their loved ones and sometimes to themselves. They can blank it out, convincing themselves that what they are doing is perfectly acceptable behaviour.

Psychiatrist Gail Saltz believes a secret life develops when the shame and guilt and the fear of consequences (real or imagined) create in you a desperate need to keep such things from becoming known. It is when the importance of the secrets starts to significantly affect your relationships that the balance of power shifts and a person is no longer in control. The secret controls them.

When you start keeping secrets from others, it isolates you. You are not who people think you are and you are the one who knows it. It is hard to maintain relationships with friends, family and partners as there will always be a sense of distrust.

Some people enjoy secrets so much that they get paid to keep them. Being a secret agent, psychiatrist or doctor requires you to be secretive to protect top secret information or patient confidentiality. Most jobs do have a level of confidentiality required, including lawyers, bankers, nurses, government employees, and a priest will respect a person's desire to keep something a secret.

Did you know that secrets can make you sick? It is the view of psychiatrist Gail Saltz that secrets can carry a hidden price that affects both our psychological and physical health.

- Some people keep their mental health issues a secret due to social stigma about the subject and not wanting to bring shame on their family or themselves. Left untreated this can be tragically damaging to their emotional stability and also damaging to their personal relationships.
- Keeping secrets can provoke an inner conflict which in turn can result in endless worry and anxiety. These are both well known to carry health implications.
- High levels of stress due to maintaining a secret can lead to problems such as headaches, back pain, high blood pressure and digestive problems.
- If you are prone to suffering from depression the stresses related to secrecy can make you even more vulnerable.
- If the secret is addiction ie. drugs/alcohol/eating disorder/smoking etc then the anxiety related will increase the need for self-satisfying indulgences.
- If a person hides things from themselves they are risking their health ie. if a woman decides to not deal with a lump in her breast or someone ignores the fact they have an unhealthy lifestyle they are secretly avoiding dealing with the situation.

Indications that you or someone you know is keeping a secret which may have health implications are:

- Displaying emotional distress without an apparent cause is a sign of keeping something from yourself or someone else.
- Feelings of increased anxiety, sadness or depression are a sign there is something shameful being hidden or fear to admit something.
- Angry outbursts, exhaustion or physical complaints for no significant reason can suggest that someone is dealing with stress related to keeping secrets.

If you have a secret that you are not willing to disclose but you are hoping to deal with, there is something you can do about it. It is all about self-exploration. Allow yourself to feel and deal with the emotions and memories involved in dealing with your secret. Allowing yourself to understand the hows and whys will help you to deal with the situation internally. This can be done through therapy, meditation or any other way you feel comfortable.

I would like to stress that the health benefits of a happy marriage and happy relationships are widely known, so being open and honest with yourself and others is not only a happier way to live, it is a healthier way to live which will add years to your life. Let's all be more open with each other and live longer for it.

Happiness

What does happiness mean to you? Do you feel happy regularly? Did you know that by feeling happy you are attracting more happiness into your life?

We all experience an abundance of emotions daily and hopefully happiness is one that we all allow ourselves to experience. Yes, we decide if we are going to be happy or not. It is in our control to do so. Our minds determine the feelings we experience so if we take the time to re-programme our minds to appreciate simple everyday things, thus making us happier within, it will ultimately lead us towards a happier life. Hey, we have nothing to lose so why not try it?

Different things make people happy because we are all unique individuals with many different focuses and desires.

"Every human being on the planet wants to be happy. Anything that anyone desires is because they think their desire will make them happy. Whether it is health, money, a loving relationship, material things, accomplishments, a job or anything at all, the desire for happiness is the bottom line of all of them. But remember that happiness is a state inside of us, and something on the outside can only bring fleeting happiness, because material things are impermanent. Permanent happiness comes from you choosing to be permanently happy. When you choose happiness, then you attract all the happy things as well. The happy things are the icing on the cake, but the cake is happiness." Rhonda Byrne

Happiness can be categorised into groups:

Scientific: I was fascinated to discover whilst researching happiness that many studies have concluded that money, education or weather do not have the positive effect on our true happiness we all have come to believe. Psychologist Mark Seligman has summarised that humans seem happiest when they have incorporated in their lives, pleasure (warm baths, good foods, etc), engagement, positive relationships, meaning and accomplishments. He also says that from a mental health point of view there is evidence that people can empower themselves to improve their own happiness.

Religion: People's inner spiritual belief system can lead to ultimate happiness as they entrust their own personal joy to a higher being. In Buddhism happiness is the central theme of their teachings and is believed to be a state of everlasting peace. Catholics believe blessed happiness awaits at the ultimate end of each human's time on Earth as God's essence is there in the next life. No matter what religious or spiritual belief an individual has, the aim is the same: people strive for happiness.

Philosophical: Many great thinkers offer different variations on the meaning of happiness but they all agree that it comes from within and can only be accessed by the individual's desire to experience it.

Aristotle has stated that happiness is the only thing that humans desire for their own sake, unlike the desires of riches, honour, health or friendship as these were sought in order to be happy.

Happiness is a characteristic of a good life. It is said the happy person is more virtuous, which indicates unimaginable abilities and emotional tendencies enabling us to fulfil our common human ends.

"Happiness is the virtuous activity of the soul in accordance with reason." Aristotle.

Being part of a community or group, whether it is a physical presence or online, is a very powerful way to feel happy as you are interacting with people you choose to spend time with and that can only lead to increasing your level of happiness. That is why positive, happy websites like adopt-a-mum which focuses on offering loving support and building beautiful bonds for all its members is a wonderful resource in the pursuit of happiness.

I choose happiness every day and right now I am having a 'happy moment'. My children are playing happily in the garden as I sit here and write this article. I choose to appreciate these simple yet happier moments that are sent to me and so I am happier for it.

However you decide to be happy it is worth trying to pursue happiness as it has been widely known that it ultimately leads to a much longer and more prosperous life.

Happiness exercise:

If you are not happy right in this moment I would like to challenge you to STOP! Take a moment to think of a happy thing, something you enjoy doing or something that has happened that made you feel happy or laugh.

Now close your eyes and just feel it; let the feeling be absorbed so that it reaches your inner core. Hold it there for however long you want. Now any time you feel unwanted emotions, replace them with the happy one. Think happy thoughts and they will come back to you.

Our outer glow

While researching auras for my debut novel I developed an increased fascination for the whole essence of them. Better understanding your aura may help you in the quest to better understand yourself. I love that I have learned there is no aura described as bad.

The aura is described as an energy field. It can be seen by gifted psychics but more practically by using a special camera called a Kirlian Camera. This takes a photograph that captures the vibrant colours that surround an individual due to the energy they create.

It is believed each of these vibrant colours has a significant meaning which is linked to an individual's personality and character. Two main colours will usually be more prominent in the aura and are believed to be retained during a person's lifetime and even through previous lifetimes.

These views are shared by Alison Yates who wrote an article about aura colour meanings for Ezine articles:

"Aura colour can be affected by experiences in past lives and current lifetimes and can change over time depending on circumstances, general health and emotional and mental states. But, despite illness, events and circumstances, an aura usually retains the one or two dominant colours throughout life."

Psychics believe that it is through these two dominant colours that a path can be predicted to determine an individual's fortune.

However it is possible for an individual's dominant colours to change and this can be linked with a deep and meaningful spiritual journey, thus changing a person's core values and personality traits.

Having studied different views of the main vibrant aura colours and their meanings, here is what I have concluded for each colour:

RED: Stamina , physical energy, spontaneity and life force. Described as easily bored with people and/or projects, so can tend to move on easily. However if an interest is held and maintained, success and wealth can prevail. Quite straightforward individuals with nothing to hide.

ORANGE: Creative, sensitive and optimistic. Described as being sensitive to others' emotions, thus leaving people feeling at ease in their company. Can have the urge to achieve and be proudly self-sufficient and are known for leading a successful and happy life.

GREEN: Harmony, popular, admiration and respect. They are capable of being very successful in business and at creating wealth. Things are well thought out before being acted upon and they enjoy a sense of balance and security in their lives.

BLUE: Organised, motivational and communication. They are known to be strong in character and born leaders by conveying their thoughts charismatically. This aura colour is quite rare to see.

PURPLE: Spiritual, psychic and intuitive. Known to be tuned to others' moods and emotions. They are born to learn about a wide range of subjects so are widely knowledgeable, which can make them very interesting people. Although they can also be perceived as being mysterious or secretive.

SILVER: Opportunistic, adaptable and blessed. They are known to be high in intellect, which enables quick thinking and actions. Easily successful as they are talented and very lucky in life.

GOLD: Good listeners, charming and generous. They are known to be attractive to others and enjoy attention and admiration from others but they will also give attention equally. They are often very popular people and make great friends.

WHITE: Angelic, spiritual and evolved. They are known to be highly spiritually evolved and close to God. They also incorporate qualities from all of the other colours.

There is also a process called Chakra clearing which could be beneficial to any individual who often has numerous hardships or bad luck in general. This can be done by yourself at home in the bath or shower. Chakras are internal energy points which can be used to release unwanted energies. There are six internal points that need clearing. These points are: the head, the throat, the heart, upper abdomen, below the naval and the V at the bottom of your torso (top of your legs) - this is the root base of your chakra.

"Despite all best efforts, no amount of external clearing can really clear the internal core of our own chakras. This release technique is very powerful for it empowers you (or the individual you are assisting) to actively participate in the energetic clearing of all the chakras."

The cycle of life

Take a moment to think about your life until now. Has your life gone through cycles? You are going to find out and maybe experience a few 'Aha!' moments when doing so. Just as the universe has the universal law of attraction that is relevant to us all, it also has the law of cycles.

Think of it like this. There are times in our lives when we instigate something important to us. It may not happen as we want it to and often people say, "It was not the right time" and they are right. By understanding the law of cycles you will understand when is the best time in your life to embark on a mission to have a maximum positive effect on your life. It is like a seed. When you plant a seed you make sure the ground is prepared and it is the right time of the year for that seed to flourish. By applying the same care and attention to your own personal thought process and the ventures you undertake, it will ultimately lead to you reaping higher rewards for your hard work.

Your personal number

We all have our unique birth date. That date is significant to each of us individually as it is used in determining which year of the nine-year cycle you are currently travelling in.

The process to follow is quite simple and you do not need to be a top mathematician to work it out, so don't worry. Grab a piece of paper and a pen.

How to calculate your personal cycle number for this year:

(D+D+M+M+Y+Y+Y+Y = _) then (_ + _ = _)

If you want to find out what your birth number was when you were born just change the year. Easy!

* Most numerologists believe that each cycle year begins on the New Year. There are others who believe that each year of the cycle begins on your birthday. I feel that individually we know when there is a shift in our cycle.

The Nine Year Cycle

Each year is another portion of the pie of life. However each will bring different conditions and energies our way. By understanding each part of the cycle you will be creating a deeper understanding of yourself and your place in your life, ultimately empowering yourself to be in the right place at the right time.

Year 1: New beginnings. This is the time for a new beginning, whether it be training, a new job, self-discovery, a relationship, new thinking. Be confident and embark on this new journey. It is a great time for planning your future. Preparing the ground for planting.

Year 2: Planting the seed. Now that you know what your focus is on during this cycle of your life it is time to build the foundations which will secure your future success. Building strong relationships and researching. Patience is the key.

Year 3: Leave it to do its magic. It is time to let the seed do its work, time to have fun. You will see and feel that things are growing because of the previous two years' preparations. Nervous excitement and energy will be high. However, the seed has not grown yet! Enjoy your surroundings and experience more as the horizons widen. Not a good time to start new relationships as the focus is on other things.

Year 4: Taking Root. An important year when more hard work is required. The roots of your seed are taking place so it is a time to ensure that it keeps growing. A year to stabilise and keep everything in order to ensure success keeps growing. Full attention and concentration needed, be practical. Further investment may be needed. Do not take anything for granted at this point.

Year 5: Results. Your hard work is showing signs of paying off as it shoots up out of the ground. More opportunities come your way to enhance growth potential. Freedom is the feeling you should be experiencing. A time to constructively move away from old routines towards newer, fresher experiences.

Year 6: Nurturing. Obligation to your responsibilities this year. Also a time to appreciate the previous years and any assistance you received. A time of abundance as things really are growing so appreciate that.

Year 7: Be grateful for growth. This year you have the opportunity to be grateful for the successes of the previous years. This is a year of inner reflection and understanding of the process thus far. Ask yourself questions - what have you learned? What could you do better next cycle? An important year of reflection. It is also a lucky year!

Year 8: The flower blooms. This year of the cycle reveals its beauty. Abundant rewards are there for the taking. The more you have put in, the more you will receive this year. New opportunities will present themselves and the winds of change will start to blow.

Year 9: Reflection. This year is the time when we move on and discover inner peace. Absorb the wisdom and use this year as a time to reflect on everything you have learned in order to create a better understanding of the process. Enjoy this time of personal realignment in preparation for the next new beginning.

I am excited about the possibilities of numerology, not only personally but for my children. As a mum I will be able to easily monitor which year of the cycle they are in and with this information I can help guide them through life, enabling them to plan a brighter future.

Having an introduction to the nine-year cycle, do you feel that life will be easier and more relaxed for you? Will you be able to plan and understand the future better?

Law of Loving Attraction

The Spiritual Law of Love

Over the past few years I have become increasingly fascinated with the whole concept of metaphysics or *The universal law of attraction,* which is the term most of us are more familiar with. I began to explore and embrace affirmations, especially those of Louise Hay, who has guided many people gently through the process of transforming their thoughts to assist in bettering their lives and healing themselves physically and emotionally.

Then there is the phenomenon of *The Secret* by Rhonda Byrne. This book and movie really connected with me. It is more of a factual guidance that reveals something fascinating and intriguing. The power of our thought and the history behind the power of this knowledge really sparked something inside me and I started to implement conscious thought processes in my life to test if it worked.

As I am a spiritual person and have made a transformation within that has connected deeply with my inner spirit, I knew any conscious alterations in my thought process would also have to complement the peace and fulfilment I have achieved through my inner connection.

I started off small. If my day was not flowing well, I would stop for a short time and readjust my thoughts to a more positive mindset. Every time I did this my day would change towards being a more positive and enjoyable experience. The energy I was putting out there was the energy I was receiving.

I also used the same principle with my children. When they were going crazy and getting on my nerves I would readjust my thoughts and remind myself they are just children who need loving guidance. By playing up and messing about they were just being healthy kids and testing their boundaries. If I responded in a furious over-reactive way, then I was affirming to them that their behaviour was acceptable as I was responding in the same way and they would then continue on their rampage. When I took a few moments to adjust my thoughts and feelings and consciously send love to them, I found that almost immediately they changed their behaviour. The same principles applied when my husband was having an off day.

The point I am making is that immediately in that one moment I was able to apply simple changes that made a positive difference in MY life.

I put together a vision board and events began presenting themselves to me that led me towards achieving my dreams. I discovered that part of the process of receiving everything we want from life is to be open and aware of the opportunities that came our way after we request something, whilst also using our heart and being guided by our inner spirit as to whether the choices we are making are right for us.

Spirituality

If we ask for something and things shift to enable us to receive it and our heart is affirming that it is right for us, then don't deprive yourself. It is right for you! Our inner spirit is our guide and it will not allow us to drift too far off our path without letting us know.

When we as individuals connect with our inner spirit we activate our strongest intention. When we connect this intention with our desire for something to manifest, whether it be emotional, spiritual, material or any other medium, we activate our strongest power.

Passion

When we approach things with a true glowing passion we will receive far more quickly. A lot of things I do, I do with passion and a whole-hearted true intention. Things happen for me very quickly. I discovered I was passionate about becoming a writer. In two and a half years I have written two novels, more than sixty articles and set up a rapidly growing publishing business — and all of this whilst being a mum to four. Every single step of each moment. I am now finishing my third novel and my heart is singing. I was guided towards what I needed to do in this process.

Negative influences

I have come to realise, through my own experiences and other interactions I have witnessed that the people we connect with regularly can have a huge impact on our mood and therefore influence our thoughts and life outcomes. Do you put up with a negative influence in your life because the person is a family member or you work closely with them or for some other reason? If you do I strongly advise that you try your best to limit, as much as possible, any interactions with them. If this seems impossible then try your best to make any interactions with that person more positive.

You can also consciously create an energy shield around yourself to block out the toxic energies this person projects by taking a moment to centre yourself within. Doing this will create a stronger centre of balance for you. Follow that by imagining you have a protective shield around your whole body and nothing this person says or does will alter the way you are feeling right now. Keep yourself conscious that you are not going to let your feelings be altered by the negative influences the other person expresses.

Religion and attraction

Many people access their ability to attract things through their religious practice. Prayer is very powerful as often it is not only one person, but many people, all focusing on the one outcome for themselves or another. There are many different religions, all of which can influence the power of thought through their practice.

By watching the movie *The Secret* I realised the power of combined, focused thought is covenanted as it has the potential to alter the pattern of life for us all, it is that strong.

When large groups of people get together with the same passion and intention the energy emitted is on a transforming level and the universe must do its job in responding. This is not only the case in religion but also for worldwide campaigns, rallies where a lot of people gather together for the same cause. The internet can reach so many and the energy combined from all over the globe at a specific time has monumental potential to shift energy frequencies.

Loving Law of Attraction: The Mirror Effect

Stop for one moment! Think about what you are doing. What type of energy are you projecting? What do others see and experience from you? The only way to know this is to look in the mirror. This simple act will allow you to experience the outer you that others experience all the time.

You will be fascinated to know that looking at yourself in the mirror is one of the hardest things for a lot of people.

Love Yourself.... Do you love yourself? If you don't truly love yourself (warts and all), then how can you expect someone else to love you? Can you honestly look in a mirror and say to yourself "I love you!" with all of your heart? This simple act can turn out to be one of the most liberating things you will ever do in your lifetime.

Louise Hay affirms that this is one of the most wonderful things you can do for your self-love. Jack Canfield, author of the *Chicken Soup for the Soul* series, often talks about 'The Mirror Exercise'. It is a self-love exercise that is designed to be completed every night.

Give it a go...
- Get ready for bed.
- Stand quiet and alone for a few minutes.
- Find a mirror and stand in front of it.
- Really look at yourself, deep into your eyes. It may feel awkward at first but try to stick with it, it will get easier the more you do it.

- Examine yourself closely. Your eyes, your skin, your forehead, your nose, your mouth, your body (if the mirror is big enough); examine everything and try to only think positive thoughts about yourself. (If you are brave enough to try it naked, go for it! If not then don't pressure yourself because you can still get powerful results).
- When you are ready, look lovingly into your eyes and tell yourself 'I love you' and add your name. This may make you feel uncomfortable at first and don't be hard on yourself if it does. Honour your emotions by letting them be and when you are ready, later on you can reflect on them and release them. It is important to do this because every time you do, you heal an old wound.
- Reflect on your day and think of at least five things that you appreciate yourself for and say them out loud to yourself. They can be as small or big as you like but they must be positive.
- Connect to your loving core and flow love and compassion towards yourself the best that you can. When you truly open your heart you will fell this physically like a ripple or rush in your heart.
- Focus on the things you love about yourself and tell yourself about them. Think of your reflection as your best friend who needs to hear some positives right now. We are all our own best friends and when we take time out to realise that, magic can happen.
- To finish, look deeply into your eyes (the gateway to your core) and say "I love you" and mean it

with all of your heart. Again, embrace the feelings this brings to the surface and see this process as a strength.

When you love yourself for who you are - not wanting to be someone else, just doing all that you can to be your 'best self' - you will make mountains move in your life!

This reminds me of when I was training to be a community drama tutor. At one of the workshops, we all walked around a room and when the facilitator said stop, we had to stop and stare into the eyes of the person closest to us. I could not believe my reaction, and neither could the other participants. I had come to know everyone really well over the duration of the course. We had been going away to different locations all over Ireland and Northern Ireland for almost a year together, we were cast together in plays and were working very closely. I was one of the super confident ones. I would be the one having the fun and leading a lot of the groups.

This workshop was the biggest challenge for me. I found myself closing my eyes, blinking or giggling and looking away - anything to hide my utter discomfort with the activity. I couldn't do it. I couldn't let anyone look deep. I think I could more easily have run around the room naked! Why?

Of course, looking back now I know all of the answers but at the time, I didn't. I may have always been the popular one and the joker but that was all a charade for what was going on inside, and that was a lot at this time. I didn't loathe myself but I certainly didn't love myself the way I should and I didn't want anyone to see the true me by looking so deep. It felt as though I was being invaded, it was really uncomfortable. I learned a lot about myself through this exercise. Would you have been able to let someone look into your eyes? Could you look deeply into someone else's?

Just like the mirror, what you give out is what you will receive in return! It is the Law of Attraction and when you execute it with all of the love in your open heart, this is when you will experience the all-powerful Spiritual Law of Attraction. It makes you shine your divine light out into the world so that you will attract divine magnificence into your life.

Loving Law of Attraction: A tortoise or a hare?

We have all heard the story about the hare and the tortoise. The hare brazenly boasts that there is no way in the world a tortoise could beat him in a race. This is to his own peril as his cockiness was soon proved to be his downfall. Of course the moral of this story is that being steadily consistent until the end will overcome the fast show-off hands down. We have all heard it. 'Slow and steady wins the race.'

The hare got brazen and was filled with ego whereas the tortoise was humble and consistent. For me, the tortoise is way more likeable than the hare. Who do you choose? Neither of them considered at any point that they would not reach the finish line, but the hare expected to come first. The tortoise didn't, he didn't mind the prospect of not winning but was happy when he did.

Which do you think would win a marathon? Endurance or speed? A car wastes more petrol when it speeds around, stopping suddenly and speeding off again at traffic lights and roadblocks. It may even lose control if the driver is not paying enough attention on the road ahead and the situation. Think about it; this process can also be applied to how we approach life, love, relationships, jobs, challenges...

"Going slow may not be as exhilarating a ride but it will always get you to the finish line."

When I sat down to write my first novel, if I had started with the intention of blasting out as many words as

I could, I would have ran out of steam. Instead I made it to the daily recommended word count and each day I still had inspiration to keep going until I made it over the line thirty days later. Applying this to other aspects of my life, I know that when I blast into something, I quite often hit a brick wall. When I embark on the task with a realistic goal in mind, I take each step knowing I am one step closer and wiser.

Maybe the pace of the tortoise doesn't work for everyone, I certainly can't ever imagine the hare going at the same pace as the tortoise, it would not be in its nature; but in life we can train ourselves to slow down.

Pros and cons of being a tortoise: At the tortoise's speed the exhilaration of the race is not at the same level as the hare's but the tortoise has the opportunity to enjoy the journey, not just the finish line. The tortoise gets it all...he gets to bring his home with him and yet still take part in the race.

Pros and cons of being a hare: Fulfilment can be harder to achieve and the next race is never far away. Always after the goal, never enjoying the journey.

I used to live my life at the hare's speed; I was always exhilarated but never fulfilled! Life decided to give me a jolt that made me live one day at a time and since then I have lived at the pace of a tortoise. I now have time to look around me and embrace life as I still pursue a finishing line; it is so much more fulfilling. I have, on occasion, noticed the hare try to sneak back in, trying to coax me to run again, and sometimes I do for a while but nothing beats the tortoise's pace for me!

There are jobs that require fast thinking and action and that is fine once balance is found in other areas. Life goes fast for many of us. Sometimes if we don't keep up we may feel like we will be left behind but I can assure you that if you keep making progress towards your goal, no matter the pace, you will catch up with the hares at some point because they will have to stop to rest.

In relevance to the Law of Attraction, if you live the fast- paced life all of the side effects that come with that will come at a fast pace too and your body may begin to suffer as a result (something worth considering).

Are you a tortoise or a hare?

What would you prefer to be?

Karen Weaver

Loving Law of Attraction: Ask – Believe – Receive

You can be whatever you want to be.

"Life is not so much about finding yourself as it is about creating you."

Why is it that as children we are encouraged by our parents, storytellers and society to dream and believe that anything is possible, only to be drawn away from this momentum as we move into adulthood? Why is it, as adults, many of us turn our back on the magic of life to embrace a more socially acceptable, duller reality as we advance through the years? Is it all a process? There are those who are lucky enough to reconnect with their inner child at some point during their journey, and this more carefree, fun approach to life can bring about a more enjoyable experience of existence during this lifetime. I am not saying we should all start acting like children, but we can learn a lot from connecting on a more consistent basis with the magical dreamy believer – our inner child.

Take a step back!

Take a step back for a moment to look at what you have become in the now and momentarily ask yourself, 'Are you happy with who you are?' Does your heart sing from time to time, reminding you that your body, mind and spirit are aligned? Do you feel fulfilled? If the answer is no to any of these questions, then what have you got to lose if you consider opening yourself to alternative possibilities? This does not have to be a dramatic life-changing event. It may simply be doing something that you hadn't considered before and discovering you actually like it; or promising yourself to save some special time just for you at the end of every day; or even beginning to take steps towards fulfilling a personal goal. Each little positive step can soon become a momentous positive journey.

Get rid of that mental block!

Think about something you would really like to have in your life, something that will enhance your experience of life but won't jeopardise anything precious that you already have. Believe it is possible for you to fulfil the dream of receiving whatever it is. Think about it often; make yourself feel like you already have it. Think of it as mentally preparing yourself for receiving. Make it real in your mind and feel it wholeheartedly and you will make it real in your reality. Do not let doubt create a blockage in your mind; have a clear vision and let the light shine on it.

ANYTHING IS POSSIBLE, YOU JUST HAVE TO BELIEVE!

Attraction

By truly believing, you will attract opportunities that will help you create your best future. It is important to become more aware of signs and when opportunity comes knocking, answer the door! Be mentally prepared to be brave and take the plunge towards your heart's desire. People around you will start to believe in your dream when they begin to witness what you are attracting your way. You need to believe in order to attract, that is your job in the process. All you have to do is be aware and don't turn your back on the opportunities that will help you make your desire a reality. If you turn your back on these opportunities then how are you supposed to take the next step along the journey of receiving? It is a process and we all have some work to do to achieve. If we choose not to then we don't want it enough or it is not right for us. Regret is not an option. If it is meant to be, the opportunity will find its way to us again.

"Do your best with what you have now and it will attract more to you in the future."

My attraction

I live the perfect life for me. I know the Law of Attraction is hard at work for me every single day. I know that I have attracted to me everything good, and even some of the not so good. I love that I have the power to influence my own life in the way I choose. My life may not be what someone else would choose for themselves, nor may it have turned out exactly as I thought it would, but because I have always remained open and followed what I felt was right for me it has paid off and I am living my dream. I would always advise anyone to stay true to themselves when they are feeling confused about what road to take. Connect with your intuition, it will guide you! And when you know what it is that you want, then put it out there and act on every opportunity that you possibly can that will bring that desire one step closer to reality. I am very grateful for everything I have been blessed with, I treasure it wholeheartedly!

Be your own Master

It is good to remember that we are the masters of our own life. It is a life we have been gifted with by a higher source, a source that will bring to us our mind's requests. When our requests come from a positive loving place, what we receive will also be positive and loving and vice versa.

The Law of Attraction, when consciously connected to our inner spirit, can be a strong generous amalgamation of power that can work to meet our highest potential. When we allow our heart to sing and have faith, that is when our heart's desires will be delivered. Anything is possible!

We cannot control everything that occurs in our lives but we can control how we choose to react to it. Try to remain conscious in every moment and to pause before a reaction, because nothing is so urgent that it need not take a moment to address. The moment to address action can be used to instigate a response through a loving heart and with the truest of intention only the purest outcome will ensue, if that is how we choose to live our life.

"When we live our life through love we are choosing to live our best possible life."

By living a life of passion we attract those desires to us at a faster pace because when we live with passion, we feel with passion and the universe provides us with what we are most passionate about.

It is a must to focus our passionate energy on what it is we want to manifest the most.

Think it, feel it and believe it!

Loving Law of Attraction: A negative path

It is important to understand that just as you can attract many positive things into your life, you can attract negative things too. This can be an overwhelming responsibility of thought for many of us, but it is a fact. The way we can help control it is through our feelings. A chain of events that happened to me instigated this thought process.

I began to feel an energy shift and instead of dealing with it as I usually would, by doing something nice for me that makes me feel good such as writing, spending some time with friends or going for a walk, I found myself being consumed by a strong unsettling feeling. This unsettling feeling was picked up on by my very in-tune friends at Soul Sistas Healing as cards began jumping out at them with messages for me. I then requested a reading that stated someone would slyly betray my trust. Of course my mind went into overdrive. Before I knew it I had conjured up all sorts of scenarios in my over-active imagination (attracting allsorts to me), but the main thing was that a gloomy shadow of negative feelings engulfed me and it would not shift. I just didn't have the strength to shift it – I was tired and doing a lot. So I chose not to react, I chose to let it pass over. Whatever it was going to be, I was going to have to deal with it, I had reached a level of acceptance. Once it didn't physically affect any of my family I didn't mind, I could deal with it. I began to simplify things around me for the short term.

The next day my husband phoned to tell me he had had an accident on the freeway but no one was hurt. I was so relieved.

The negative sensation was still there, yet dimmer than before. A few days later my negative emotion and the negative journey of another crossed paths. My Cash Card was stolen and the person went on a shopping spree. I don't usually have cash in my account like that but circumstances following the incident a few days earlier had led to there being money in my account and that person was guided to it. Also the shops he visited facilitated his deception by not being suspicious, but then again this is the universe providing the desires of the other person.

You see, the universe had aligned all of these things to make this happen not just for me but for the opportunist that was focused on achieving their goal – with passion.

The key to conquering the situation before it accelerates to the outcome is not to over think, it is to make yourself 'over feel'! Over-feel good feelings. When we feel with passion we are manifesting things at a faster pace. We have the ability to realign! This is a power we are all born with. I know now that I should have realigned when I got the warning signals. If I had listened and acted in a positive way, all could have been avoided. I may have done one small thing that would have changed the course of this happening.

Everything happens for a reason. Sometimes we can explain why...sometimes we can't. Sometimes we need to take action....sometimes we don't. All I can recommend is that you listen to your intuition. Be aware of how you are feeling. If you are feeling unsettled then do one small thing that will accommodate a realignment and then FEEL GOOD ABOUT IT!

The Law of Attraction is all about learning. You may navigate onto a negative path, either your own or stumble onto someone else's. Either way it is worth remembering that YOU have the power to move forward at whatever pace you decide to. You have the power to choose how you deal with each scenario. You choose whether to allow someone else to dictate how you should deal with something, or you listen to your intuition and move forward more equipped with knowledge and experience to perhaps prevent similar happenings in future. Wise words state that 'prevention is better than cure' and the best way of doing this is by listening to our intuition. It is our spirit guide and it will let us know if something is wrong. It will niggle us until we listen and act. It has our best interests at its core, it works for our greater good!

Try your best to find a positive in every negative situation – there is always one if you take the time to look

"From all negative situations is the potential for a positive outcome."
Karen Mc Dermott ~ *The Visitor*

Loving Law of Attraction: To catch a fish!

No matter what you pursue in your life you will be best rewarded if you are patient. Think of the fisherman. If he wants to catch a big juicy fish he will first find out where the specific fish is positioned and then he will prepare himself for the long haul.

Picture it now…making sure he has the best bait to attract the fish to his line, and then HE WAITS! You will never see a fisherman hop into the water and make a fish bite his line. It doesn't work like that. The fisherman has in his mindset that he may have to wait all day to make the catch of the day or it may happen on the first bite. He may have to weather all sorts of storms but the one thing that never changes is his faith and belief in the possibility of the outcome. Whilst he is waiting he may imagine what it would be like to finally catch the perfect fish. Little does he know that by imagining he is manifesting.

When that bite comes, that's when all the hard work starts. Then he has to reel his fish in successfully. There may be a tango of differences during the process but when that fish is caught in the net, the exhilarating feeling that ensues is worth it. That fish is a deserved reward for the fisherman.

Yes, if you want to be a fisherman you have to focus, be patient, believe it's possible and work hard. The same rule applies for everything worth having in life.

Many times I have achieved the big catch by using this principle. When I chose to move to Australia from

Ireland, I focused on the goal. I was patient during the process (which took two years), believed with all of my heart that it could happen and that it was right for me, and then I worked really hard placing myself in the position to receive my dream (preparing, setting up and settling in). By the time I had received it, it was already a reality for me!

Now, and in my future, I continue to apply this principle to different aspects of my life because I experience the benefits it has. I love to write and I have published some of my work. The more I cast my line in the right places the more chance I have of achieving my big catch. Now that, for me, would be exhilarating.

Don't underestimate the process of WAITING.

We have to wait for things for a reason. Our mindset needs to adjust from dream state to reality based during the waiting period. If we received something the moment we imagined it, it would be mind-blowing! It is the time we have to believe that it is possible and the time to consider if the outcome is right for us. Are you sacrificing too much to receive? Is there room for something new to enter your life? This is the time set aside to consider all of these things; before you receive you may need to spring clean your life to make room for it. The fisherman is sacrificing time and energy for the momentary exhilaration of the catch. He had to make room for that time but what is he missing out on? Was it worth it?

This process of attraction can also work for negative thoughts too. If you focus your energy on something that you don't want to attract and you believe that it is possible, you are indeed working against your greater good. Always try your best to focus on a positive outcome!

Finally...DONT GIVE UP! When you 'Put it out there' be open to every possibility of it coming to you. Just like the fisherman catching his big catch, he cannot control when that is going to happen. He can put himself in the best position, be prepared for any scenario and be willing to wait it out!!

"Good things come to those who wait...and believe...and think positive...and are prepared to work hard."

The answer is 'LOVE'

What is the question? What is the key to true happiness?

We all strive to be happy. No matter what circles we revolve in, our main goal is happiness. Whether it is materialistic or ambitious our end goal is achieving something that makes us, as individuals, feel happy.

Many people strive for perfection. But who is it that determines what perfection is? We all have our own ideals of perfection and aim for that, and why? To make us HAPPY!

Now armed with this information that feeling love makes us happy, what are you going to do about it? How do you get enough love to make you happy? I am pleased to tell you that you don't need to go seeking it; you just need to unlock the vault to your own self love. By loving ourselves we will discover true happiness that no amount of materialistic possessions will ever give us. When we access this love we will discover there is a never-ending supply all for ourselves that we can share with others and it will never dry up. In fact the more we spread our love, the more that is created and the more that comes back to us.

I like to think of it as a snowball. By starting off with a little ball of love and giving it the opportunity to grow by rolling it along and nurturing it, we enable it to become a greater ball of love. Then in no time at all it will be ready to roll down the mountain of life gathering more and more love all of the time. What do we have at the end? A great BIG ball of Love that everyone can feel and enjoy.

Did you know we can heal our body and mind just by loving ourselves? Simply by taking the time to listen to the signals your body is giving, you have the power within you to perform miraculous things.

"Love creates miracles, Love creates magic."
Sascha Brooks

Louise L. Hay is a very inspiring woman and she passionately expresses how by loving yourself and affirming this love through positive affirmations you can heal ANY ailment or illness you may have. Yes, it is that amazing!

Tips on how to love yourself

Self-love may sound easy to do, but it is a process that needs focus and time to blossom. People who have suffered childhood neglect and abuse will find it very difficult to take the steps towards self-love. Here are some tips I came across to assist in overcoming these steps.

- Compile a list of things OTHERS like about you. Ask people who know and love you what they like about you. This is a first step towards realising your personal qualities.

- Write your own list of what YOU like about yourself. Be honest to yourself. If you are having trouble, think about the people you love and the qualities you admire in them. Do you have those same qualities?
- Feel good notebook/box. Invest in a notebook or box that makes you feel good when you see it. Use it to keep these lists. Look at its contents every time you feel low or if you are made to feel low by someone else.
- Read as much as possible. Make reading these wonderful things about you a regular occurrence in your life as often as you can. Every time you do, it will eliminate one time you felt bad or were made to feel bad and replace it with a positive.
- Add a note. Make yourself tune in to hearing the positives about yourself, no longer the negatives. Write each of them down and add them to your collection.
- You are your own best friend. We all love our friends but I have news for you: YOU are your own best friend. Love yourself as you do your friends. Close your eyes, feel the love you have for them and project it onto yourself. Store that feeling.
- Give yourself a break. Learn to be compassionate and forgiving to yourself. Would you be so hard and judgmental on your friends or loved ones? No, you would probably be there

offering support. Feel that love and compassion for yourself.

- Love comes from within. A well of love exists within us all and we can access it whenever we choose. Access self-love regularly. You deserve to be loved, so love yourself.
- Affirmations. By using affirmations you are registering positives in your brain which will help you to feel good. Things like: *I am an amazing, loving and caring person. I deserve the very best in my life. I am a loving and caring person.* Pin them up in the areas you are in most often – car, computer, fridge, work. Feel them.
- Nurture yourself. Do things for yourself that make you feel loved and cared for. A nice pampering session, some meditation, a wonderful book, a peaceful walk. These are some things we can gift to ourselves that will enhance our loving potential.
- Listen. Take a quiet moment to listen to yourself and the signs you are receiving. It may take time to connect but by giving yourself some time each day to listen to your inner guide you will more easily recognise your needs and desires.
- Look. This will be a hard one for many. I know it was for me. Look in a mirror; look straight into your eyes and tell yourself "I love you". Do this every day as often as you feel comfortable with and you will find it will get easier. I found it very emotional the first time I did

it. For me the eyes are the gateway to the soul and I felt an intense feeling at that moment.

These are all tips you can use to assist on your journey to self-love. You need only select those you feel will work for you. It can be hard to give yourself this gift at first but always know that you have the courage and strength within you and you deserve it!

The love you attract from others comes from you initially. If you don't love yourself then it is really hard for others to love you. I know this because I went through a period where I did not take the time to love me. I was just motoring along, loving my family and doing what I thought was right. But it wasn't OK. My relationships were straining around me and I was not being fulfilled, my soul was perishing. Since learning to love myself I radiate love and in every aspect of my life all of my relationships have blossomed too. I have so much love now within and I know that I will always glow.

When I talk about loving myself I don't mean being arrogant; this is when someone thinks only of them. No, self-love is when someone has a strong sense of respect for and confidence in themselves. This is usually taught in childhood through honesty, acceptance and unconditional love. However most parents have their own issues of self-doubt and limiting beliefs which they project onto their children consciously and unconsciously and so a cycle of self-rejection repeats itself.

So let's break the cycle and the stigma attached to self-love. In order to truly love another we need to love ourselves first. It is important not only for us but for our families and for humanity. Everything in life will be better now that we know 'The Answer'.

"Love is the great miracle cure. Loving ourselves works miracles in our lives." Louise L Hay

Through the Darkness

Why it is important to embrace life's spiritual struggles

"If there is no struggle, there is no progress."
Fredrick Douglass

It is really important to embrace life's struggles. Just as we embrace the good times we must also learn to embrace and move forward from the tough times. This is how we grow stronger in spirit. In the times when we find this being extra challenging I suggest a change in perspective.

Unfortunately, none of us can avoid challenges or trauma from touching our lives and instead of living in the fear of when it may come knocking on your door I suggest the emotions that engulf us during this time are opportunities for our spirits to learn how certain situations affect us. Everyone is different and everyone reacts differently to experiences. What I am encouraging is that when something deeply affects us, we embrace the emotion and learning potential of the situation. It is important to be aware and take time to recognise the lesson in every struggle. It is then we can grow in spirit and move forward stronger.

When I experienced a miscarriage a few years ago the grief consumed me. I felt the physical pain of it and it brought me to my knees. A few years previously, my granny, who I loved dearly, passed away and although I was sad about her passing I could deal with the emotion of that grief in a more rational way. I was in a different emotional place at the time of each situation. I had never before confronted how loss would affect me. In my personal experience, I learned nothing from not embracing the feelings of grief that I should have expressed the time my granny died. But when I struggled and embraced the grief I felt when I lost my pregnancy, it was so hard for me to endure but I learned so much about myself and it was the first step of my spiritual journey.

"Never let go of hope. One day you will see that it all has finally come together. What you have always wished for has finally come to be. You will look back and laugh at what has passed and you will ask yourself... How did I get through all of that?"

Author unknown

Struggle is often internal, a battle with our spirit. Working through it will make us stronger of spirit and more prepared for future struggles. Each struggle brings us closer to enlightenment and when life nears its end it is enlightenment that is our greatest wealth. We cannot bring money with us but we do bring our enlightened spirit when we leave our physicality, all lessons learned.

When we struggle and learn, we often do not have to endure the same lesson again ~ unless we did not embrace the learning in the first instance. In that case it may be tougher to endure a second time around. However, if we embrace the opportunity to grow when it first arises rather than suppress unwanted feelings, then we will be able to move forward with more ease when we encounter similar issues in our future.

I have been reading *The Five Stages of the Soul* by HR Moody as research for my third novel. In this wonderfully thought-provoking book it highlights that one of the important stages of the soul is *The Struggle* but that if embraced, the next stage of the process is *The Breakthrough*. I believe this is significant in having faith that all will be well when we endure the hardship of a struggle. There truly is light at the end of the tunnel, all we must do is follow through and reach the tunnels end. I have endured struggles of my spirit during my life thus far and I am sure that I will endure many others but when I face them now I am more aware of the potential each struggle has to gift to me.

Have you ever heard the struggling butterfly parable?

When I first read this story it clicked something within me. Something was clearer.

The story has many versions but the wisdom there is to behold from each variation is the same. Imagine the beauty of a butterfly as it flutters about radiantly from flower to flower, bringing joy to the hearts of many by its sheer beauty and elegance. But before it reaches the stage of becoming a butterfly, it is a caterpillar who slugs along desperately munching as much as it can because it is guided in the 'knowing' that this is what it is supposed to do to reach its highest potential. Becoming a butterfly is the divine path for the butterfly but it must struggle through many junctures to reach that stage.

The Butterfly Story

One day a man found a cocoon of a butterfly. A small opening appeared and he sat and watched the butterfly for several hours as it struggled to force its body through that little hole. Then it seemed to stop making any progress. It appeared as if it had gone as far as it could and it could go no farther.

So the man decided to help the butterfly. He took a pair of scissors and snipped the remaining bit of the cocoon.

The butterfly emerged easily. But it had a swollen body and small, shriveled wings.

The man continued to watch the butterfly because he expected that, at any moment, the wings would enlarge and expand to be able to support the body, which would contract in time. Neither happened! In fact the butterfly spent the rest of its life crawling around with a swollen body and shriveled wings. It was never able to fly!

What the man in his kindness and haste did not understand was that the restricting cocoon and the struggle required for the butterfly to get through the tiny opening were nature's way of forcing fluid from the body of the butterfly into its wings so that it would be ready for flight once it achieved freedom from the cocoon.

Sometimes struggles are exactly what we need in our life. If we went through our life without any obstacles it would cripple us. We would not be as strong as we could have been. And we could never fly.

So maybe allow yourself to change your perspective on *The Struggle*. When you are under pressure or enduring a challenge, remember the plight of the butterfly and know you will be a better person after you have gone through it. So often in life, what seems harsh in nature is really wisdom in reality.

Healthy minds

I am a great believer in the need for us all to keep our minds healthy. Our mind is so precious and we should never take it for granted. We can all endure a lot of ups and downs throughout our lives and our minds are designed to deal with different situations in different ways. Just as we take time to take care of our bodies, we also need to ensure we take care of our minds, because when our minds become ill it is harder for us to recognise. There are no apparent visual scars, yet the illness can be life threatening.

The most common form of mental illness is depression and one in five of us will encounter it at some point in our lives. Most of us will know someone who has dealt with or who is dealing with depression. It must be remembered that depression is not a weakness, it is an illness and as with any illness, you should seek medical attention in order to make a full recovery and get the chemical balance of your brain back to the proper levels. Many people choose to ignore or try to hide their illness due to the stigma attached to mental health. But what we all need to realise is that just because you suffer depression, it does not mean you are weak. In fact some of the wisest people in history have endured depression.

Personally, I experienced Post traumatic stress. I remember the moment it kicked in, I remember the shock that rippled through my body sending signals to my brain that my current reality was to be no more. My life was going to change from that moment on and I had no choice in it. No-one could have said anything that would make me believe anything different.

I withdrew myself from my family and society. I had tunnel vision and I had to simplify my life. I could not deal with drama or anyone else's problems I had to deal with mine, slowly but surely.

I went inside of myself, somewhere I had not often visited. I have always led a heart driven life, but now I was numb. I discovered that when your heart is in shock and you no longer feel safe in your surroundings, it is a very unpredictable place to reside.

I was lucky though, I had worked in a Mental Health environment for almost 4 years and I trusted my own instinct so I took every day slowly and I did not fear what was happening. I focused purely on my children, looking back, I do not remember much from the time at all.

I do recall one major event that shook me back into feeling again. I had a miscarriage. It was the most devastating experience I ever had. I cried for days. I now understand that my tears were not just for my angel baby, they were also the tears that never were. That was just before Christmas 2007 and I discovered in February 2008 that I was six weeks pregnant. This was our big year. We got engaged, we got married, we finished building a new house, we moved our family to Australia and we had our first girl.

The tunnel was no more. I could always see the light but now I could feel its warmth again, it was the best feeling in the world to feel alive again. I had a renewed outlook on life. My enlightenment journey had begun.

What I found helped me though was focusing on what really mattered to my heart, it guided me. Also as I worked in a mental health environment I did not fear what was happening. Strangely, after the initial period of unsettlement, I had a knowing that everything was going to work out.

The one thing I know for certain is that when I was going through this shadowed time in my life, I kept moving forward with the faith that everything was happening for my greater good and ultimately it was. I would not be the person I am today, living the amazing life that I now live had I not endured this time. Why? Because it was during that time when I chose to apply for a visa to come to Australia with my family.

"In times of sadness, cry a river, build a bridge and then get over it."

It is so important to find a way to release emotion. Pent up emotion is damaging to your body and mind. Finding the way to release emotion that suits you can be life changing. It is not selfish to pursue a passion, for me it is writing. Whatever your passion might be, do more of that.

When you feel your world is falling apart

At that moment in your life when you feel as if your world is crumbling around you, find comfort in knowing that everything happens for a reason. It is always for your greater good or the greater good of someone you love.

Change is part of life, but when a dramatic change happens it can shake us to the core. During the initial stages of these types of changes our bodies actually go into a state of shock. This shock may derive from the thought of the implications the change may have on our everyday lives. It can be too overwhelming to deal with at the beginning, so it is best to try to take each moment as it comes and not think too far ahead towards any possible outcomes or consequences. Trust that everything is as it should be. The following affirmation from the wonderful Louise L Hay may help.

'All is well, everything is working for my higher good, out of this experience only good will come, I am safe.'

Evolution is part of every process. Our lives change all the time, sometimes without us really recognising that a change has occurred. The Earth we live on is constantly evolving and this is evident with every discovery scientists have made whilst studying its history. Humanity also evolves constantly; we are not like the humans that were around one million years ago and in another million years humans will not be as we are now either.

Some tips for dealing with this upheaval.

- Allow the shocking grief of the situation to release. Talk, write, shed tears, find some way of releasing it. Pent up emotion is not only detrimental for our mental wellbeing, it can also damage our body. Talk to someone; go have a fight with your pillow; cry, but make sure that you release, release, release. It is important to do this as it is the first hurdle on the process to recovery.

- Next it is time to heal. Take it slow for a time. Emotions are fragile and sensitivity may be high. Be kind to yourself. Try not to have high expectations during this time, go with the flow of life and if you let someone down, don't despair, you can make it up to them again.

- Recognise that this does not just happen to you, even though it will feel very individual. It is probably the most universal experience we will all encounter in our lives, however we all deal with it in our own unique and personal ways.

- Don't over commit yourself for a while. Actual time frames are not important as we all heal at different rates and some pain goes deeper than others. But if you listen to your body and take a moment to recognise the signs that come your way, you will be guided through your healing journey.

- When it is time, keep yourself open to the possibility that you have recovered to a level where you can start maintaining day to day routines again. There are some people who get stuck in the healing journey and are not prepared to move on but it is important to do so.

Spiritually thinking

When we think of this in a spiritual context it can help us to think outside of the box and become more accepting of why some things happen to some people and not to others.

We are all created with a spirit that guides us through life. Our spirit is unique to us. Before we are born we have already chosen exactly what experiences we want to encounter during our lifetime, both good and bad. We have decided what lessons we want to learn in order for our spirits to advance towards enlightenment. Our spirit will guide us on our journey and when the times get tough it will be our spirit that will guide us through it. We can keep our spirit strong and healthy by connecting with it on a regular basis. This is why people attend church and meditate. Even going for a walk can help you go within and connect with your inner guide. When we maintain spiritual wellbeing the tough times don't hit as hard because we have that little cushion to land on.

Grief in its many shapes and forms is one of the most emotionally challenging times in anyone's life. It can never be fully prepared for and I hope my thoughts can be a saving grace for someone sometime.

Becoming more aware

We can all take steps to becoming more aware by keeping our bodies still, especially our eyeballs, as it immediately provides access to more awareness. It is also important to pay attention to our breathing because by breathing more deeply our minds are more alert and present in the moment. Attention to breath puts attention on the mind.

When we transition from individual consciousness to universal consciousness we think beyond ourselves. We think of the picture as a whole, not just the part with us in it. When we bring ourselves to that level of thought, our consciousness expands to enable us to think more universally.

Karen Weaver

Tough times revisited

When challenging times come to visit, imposing themselves on our lives without being invited, they can change the flow of our lives. When they have the cheek to invite their companion 'emotional consequences' to come knocking on our door, it is good to remember that it is our choice whether we allow them to enter, or visit at a time when we are better prepared to deal with their stopover.

The times I found hit me the hardest were the times when I experienced tough times due to consequences arising from my own choices. I decided to look deeper to get a greater understanding and I discovered that throughout my life I chose to ignore any wrongdoings that may have had a negative impact on myself or others. I suppose this was a survival mechanism at the time as maybe I wasn't as emotionally stable as I thought I was. Goodness knows how this character trait was perceived by others.

I am happy in the knowing that my personality has evolved somewhat since then. I went through a time when vivid dreams filled with past wrong doings that I never dealt with kept recurring. It was as if my subconscious mind was letting me know that it was now time to face up to the emotions connected to these situations. It wasn't easy as I mulled through the past, reliving specific moments that came to me. As a result of this revisitation I have finally granted myself and others forgiveness. A sense of being free followed as the dark cloud I didn't really allow myself to acknowledge beforehand started to turn transparent and then disappeared.

"It's simple: When you haven't forgiven those who have hurt you, you turn your back against your future. When you do forgive, you start walking forward." Tyler Perry

It is at these times we may seek some assistance, maybe from a friend or by accessing another medium in which we can release our thoughts and progress to a new level of ourselves. Allowing access to help from another source is a powerful thing in moving on as this can help clean up the emotional debris you may leave trailing behind.

"Everyone of us gets through the tough times because somebody is there, standing in the gap to close it for us." Oprah Winfrey

If used as an opportunity to change, experiencing a time of upheaval can be turned around to being a good thing, even if it doesn't feel that way at the time. I believe there is always some good to be taken from any situation and that if you change your perception you can change the impact it may have on your life from a negative one to a positive one. It can assist us in evolving from how we were, to how we are now and towards what we may become in the future. It is all about being conscious and aware of each given opportunity.

You know the old saying, "What doesn't kill you only makes you stronger". I truly believe this is true because having now embraced these situations and dealt with them, I am able to move forward and I am free of any past shackles that once held me back. Change is all part of life. It is how we deal with it in our heads that determines whether it has a positive or negative impact on our lives.

All in all I have been fortunate enough to forgive myself and others for the negative times through my life. The ability to forgive and move on is a true gift to yourself and others. I am also in the knowing that even though it may not seem likely right now, I am confident in saying that a higher source will ensure the opportunity comes around some day when I or others can make amends. Until then I am at peace with myself and accepting of my choices as each one of them has led me to the beautiful life I now have the pleasure of living.

Heart Notes

Positively dealing with trauma

Definition of trauma: "An event or situation that causes great distress and disruption." freedictionary.com

We all may encounter a traumatic event in our lives. Almost seventy per cent of us will experience a traumatic event in our lifetime. Some people deal with trauma better than others. Why is this? I am under the understanding that if you are emotionally secure and with a positive outlook on life you are better placed in dealing with the challenges life throws your way. This may be because thoughts can be controlled better without letting them get out of control and therefore we can remain more mentally stable.

You may have heard the saying 'shaken to the core'. This expression explains how a traumatic event affects our bodies. Shock is a clinical reaction our bodies take on board when exposed to a sudden event. Our bodies are programmed to survive and when our body goes into shock it is like a trip switch on a machine, switching it off until the problem is solved. Recovery from this shutdown can take time and will be individual to each person and largely dependent on each individual's mental strength.

Trauma may occur because of a natural disaster like a hurricane, tsunami, fire, earthquake or a personal disaster such as an accident, abuse, murder or being a witness to a shocking situation. It has been widely understood that people who experience personal traumas are more likely to experience PTSD (Post Traumatic Stress Disorder) as the impact is felt more personally than if it were a trauma that affects a wider community.

We can however help ourselves by keeping our minds healthy. Having a healthy mind will be like cushioning your fall at a time of trauma.

Prepare yourself before trauma
1. Try to trauma proof your mind. If you are in a good place emotionally you will recover quicker and more successfully. You can do this in many ways.
2. Know how to make yourself happy. Those endorphins will help your mind stay healthy and will also help you recover from trauma.
3. Be aware of what may happen should you ever experience trauma. Being educated and aware of what you are going through will help you recover quicker.
4. Do not harbour suppressed emotions as these are more likely to present themselves at a time of trauma and leave more to deal with at a time when there is already enough going on. Learn to embrace your emotions as they present themselves. They are little warning signs indicating all sorts of things that need to be addressed straight away because they do not just go away.

Tips on how to deal with trauma.

When trauma occurs it can feel like your whole world is falling apart and that you no longer have full control. This can be a frightening time but there are some techniques you can use to help you feel better during this time of uncertainty.

1. Relaxation techniques. These will help with bodily tensions and anxieties as when you feel angry and anxious you will need to find a way to calm your body down. You need to give this step time to take effect. Don't give up too easily.
2. Breathing. Deep breaths through your nose right down into your abdomen will help refocus your thoughts and relax your muscles.
3. Be aware of your pattern of emotions. If you find this hard to do it is recommended by Ed and Cecelia Beckham that you invest in a notebook to note regularly how you are feeling. This will help you become familiar with your emotions and be able to recognise when they shift.
4. Go to your peaceful place where you feel the safest. Often when dealing with trauma a feeling of being unsafe and fearful can engulf the body from time to time. Find your sanctuary, whether it be somewhere internal or a physical place you go to deliberately.
5. Talk – get it off your chest. This is an effective medium in getting your innermost thoughts and feelings released. A lot of healing occurs by describing and discussing traumatic events.
6. Write. If you don't feel comfortable talking yet, then why not write. Writing can be a powerful tool in releasing thoughts and helping to express emotions.
7. Walk, have a bath, have a massage, listen to soothing music. Do anything you like to do that will relax you and release feel-good vibes to your brain which will assist in recovery.

Resilience

(The ability to recover quickly from illness, change, or misfortune).

Resilience is a natural ability that we all possess, enabling us to holistically respond and renew ourselves during and after trauma. It is the ability to change from traumatic alert response to a more calmed state with a positive vision for the future. Some examples of resilient practices are exploring our spirituality, bonding with animals or nature, creativity and art and visual arts/drama. There are many community-based practices or groups which offer these services. Some people however may want to take a different approach by using their experiences of trauma to help others who experience the same; this is also part of the healing process. By helping they are healing.

My experience

Having dealt with trauma that occurred at a time when I was mentally vulnerable, I know there IS light at the end of that dark tunnel and that I should not feel isolated and different because of my experiences. My trauma was exactly that: 'my trauma'. It was individual to my circumstances at that time in my life and caused because of someone else's behavior, so not within my control.

I was at an advantage because having worked in the mental health sector for almost four years I knew what was happening to my body and what I needed to do to nurture myself through this time of emotional upheaval.

Positively dealing with trauma can be a life-changing experience and I was fortunate enough to not need to seek medical intervention. When you don't feel in control of your own emotions/thoughts and actions it is very much advisable to seek medical assistance via temporary medication or counselling which will aid you in your recovery faster and more successfully.

Disassociated Feelings

Some people disassociate themselves with their emotions in order to manage trauma. This is a natural reaction for many; however by separating our emotions from the events we are delaying vital healing processes. This natural survival technique that our bodies automatically switch on is like going into auto pilot. When we are feeling like we are back in the driving seat it is advantageous to recognise it is a good time to start becoming familiar with these stored away emotions and dealing with them accordingly.

It is when we are well in mind that we make the right decisions in our best interests. We are thinking more rationally so any healing done in the now of the controlled mind is a lot more beneficial in the long run. Most people don't recognise this time as an opportunity to clear out our inbox, even though our minds will probably be sending us reminders to do so.

We all have ups and downs in life but when a trauma occurs as a child it can be deep rooted and always carried around, affecting each and every aspect of life as you move along. To deal with these intense traumas, which I believe can be been hidden deep within, they need to be dealt with as they present themselves.

My theory is that this is done as a survival technique by our mind and bodies as their primary function is to survive and such trauma can have detrimental effects on a developing nervous system. It is only when we are older that we have the ability to start releasing and dealing with these traumas. I talk about trauma in this sense as something that has affected a child so much that it has had an impact on their emotional development.

In this instance it is as adults that we have the ability to deal with these traumas successfully should we so wish. Often fear, denial and a desire to forget stand in the way of the healing process. But I cannot stress enough that by slowly but surely dealing with the unwanted thoughts and emotions it is like sorting out a bulging inbox; as you sort out and file away each and every item you will have a clearer, brighter perspective on things and feel so much better about life in general.

Trauma affects most of us at some point in our lives. The magnitude felt is personal and individual. We may be lucky enough to be in a positive place at the time to deal with it effectively, but this is not always the case. Some may even experience PTSD or depression. Help can be a real stepping stone in the healing process as it can eliminate emotional isolation. Accessing help is so easy these days and can be so effective. It can also be kept confidential. Here is a list of helpful links which I hope will be another positive step for those dealing with their personal trauma.

Please note. I strongly advise anyone suffering from trauma to contact a support service for further assistance as soon as possible.

Drama therapy

Drama can be used to relieve unwanted feelings. Drama Therapy doesn't cost the earth and can be easily accessed through groups where you will never be judged. It can even be used at home on your own, you just have to allow yourself to indulge and best of all, it is fun. You may feel a little uncomfortable or out of character for a while but that is all part of the therapy of drama, which helps us to let go of inhibitions and restrictions we have imposed on ourselves emotionally throughout our lives. Even though we may feel silly expressing ourselves in this way we should not. Just think about it, actors do it all the time and they have gained respect for expressing themselves dramatically. Watch any interview with an actor after they have made a film. Do they not look happy? Do they not say they had so much fun when they were acting in the film? They always comment that they did and that they learned something new and also that they felt challenged. This is the same at any level of dramatic expression.

Drama can be used as a tool to express feelings of frustration, anger or any unwanted emotion. Imagine. Instead of having the repercussions of expressing those emotions to the person responsible, you can still release them and relieve your body of that unwanted stress. Suppressed feelings do not just disappear, they lie dormant, waiting until a time when they can be expressed and sometimes they are expressed at the wrong time towards the wrong person. Accumulation of such feelings can be detrimental to a person's mental stability and also affect their natural ability to deal with life's challenges. Just try it.

At a time when you are on your own, try expressing yourself dramatically and let out some unwanted emotions. If you are worried about the neighbours, put on some music. If you feel confident enough it also helps to stand in front of a mirror to create more self-awareness by putting a picture to the emotion. Some people do not feel comfortable with that initially but it is something to work towards. Do it for yourself, not anyone else. By allowing yourself to experience drama you will embark on a voyage of self-discovery.

Sharing your story is all part of the healing process

This comment shouted at me from a page recently. Such obvious words but they resonated with me so well. I began writing in 2010 and I have not stopped. It is not a desire to have my ego given a boost, I write because every time I do, I heal and release. When I first began to write it was all very deep and intense. This was what I needed to write to share what I was going through at that time. Now, as I grow, I write differently depending on what I am experiencing and am influenced by at that given time. When I feel inspired my first instinct is to write about it.

This morning I was guided to a blog that was shared by a young Irish man who has suffered from a debilitating depression. The name of his blog is 'Depression is my friend'. I did not know what to expect when I first began to read his story but it touched me in so many ways I could never have imagined. It shows me that this young man is coming through and healing as he is sharing his story to help others. His story touched me so deeply that I offered him a chance to feature it in a book I am creating. I connected with this young man's story and courage in sharing it. I encountered a dark period in my life and as I emerged out the other side of this dark tunnel I too felt compelled to share my story to maybe touch someone who may need help and hope.

So many people are reserved about sharing their low times when, in fact, it should be encouraged. If more people were brave like Conor, I reckon the taboo about mental health would begin to be totally eradicated. It is OK to have a fragile time, it doesn't mean it is going to be like that forever. People need to know they will come through and they may even come through a happier, stronger and more empowered version of themselves.

People suffering would not feel so alone during what is a life-altering time of their lives. It takes strength in abundance to share your story with the world, but is that not what we are supposed to do? Help each other in times of need? So why do so many people feel they are unable to share? Putting these limitations on ourselves is holding back healing, an important part of the process that can free you and guide someone else.

Heart Writer

Healing the write way

"People who engage in expressive writing report feeling happier and less negative than before writing. Similarly, reports of depressive symptoms, rumination, and general anxiety tend to drop in the weeks and months after writing about emotional upheavals." James W. Pennebaker

Do you write? In a diary, a blog, on a piece of scrap paper?

The one thing I have come to appreciate most over the past few years is the healing ability of writing things down. I have discovered that it is just as, if not more, effective than talking in getting thoughts out of our heads and shared. I am sure you have heard the saying 'A problem shared is a problem halved'. Sometimes there may not be anyone there to share the problem with. We may feel we don't want the problem to be resolved by another, we just need to release it.

My theory

Many of us good-natured souls have the inbuilt ability and desire to help others with their problems and often execute wonderful solutions to help someone through the most challenging of times. Wisdom can often ooze out of our pores for all to reap the benefits when they are most in need and that is wonderful.

But when it comes to ourselves and our own challenges we can't see things as clearly because they are shadowed by emotion. When we take the time to write our concerns down we are making the problem a reality rather than a thought that can be hidden from sight and shadowed. It makes it real, it makes it something we can approach from a different perspective and possibly find the resolution to for ourselves. Writing can help us to heal.

Physical health benefits

I have always been interested in metaphysics. How the energy we create through our thoughts and emotions can impact on our lives is so fascinating to me. To know that we have the power and ability to control our energy frequencies is such an empowering prospect. Of course the physics of the body and biology are sure to be linked. Louise Hay has shown how our thoughts and emotions can have physical impacts on our bodies, from a toothache right through to cancer and heart diseases. Her book and DVD 'Heal your Life' has opened so many people up to alternative ways of dealing with illness, and to many people possibly avoiding serious illness because they are more aware of how our mind, body and spirit work in unison.

I carried out some research for this article and was fascinated when I discovered a study by Dr James W. Pennebaker, a professor at the Department of Psychology at the University of Texas. For more than twenty years he has been giving people he meets an assignment. They are asked to write down their deepest feelings about an emotional upheaval in their life for fifteen to twenty minutes a day over four consecutive days. His found that most of those who followed his simple instructions discovered their immune systems strengthened, others had their grades improve and sometimes entire lives changed.

This totally affirms my thoughts about the power of writing.

Mental health

I know firsthand that writing can help you heal your mind. A few years before I began writing I suffered from post traumatic stress. This is quite an internal experience that cannot always be seen externally, other than a possible change in social attitude, as it can often make a person withdraw from society. This was the situation in my case. I felt I had to get away from my current situation and I even went so far as to move to the other side of the world. Fortunately for me this had a positive outcome as it allowed me the space I needed to explore and reconnect with life again.

When I started writing it helped bring me back to myself. I could express things in a way that worked for me. I have shared things that I never thought I would be able to share and probably would not have shared verbally with anyone. My thoughts feel free and I feel cleansed from any undealt with emotions from the past, as writing has given me the ability to release through a different voice.

If you wish to explore the prospect of writing to heal, why not try the assignment Dr James W. Pennebaker gave to his subjects:

"Over the next four days, write about your deepest emotions and thoughts about that emotional upheaval that has been influencing your life the most. In your writing, really let go and explore the event and how it has affected you. You might tie this experience to your childhood, your relationship with your parents, people you have loved or love now, or even your career. Write continuously for twenty minutes."

These writing tips accompanied the assignment:
- Find a time and a place where you won't be disturbed.
- Write continuously for at least twenty minutes.
- Don't worry about spelling or grammar.
- Write only for yourself.
- Write about something extremely personal and important for you.
- Deal only with events or situations you can handle now.

Writing has changed my life. I embrace it so much because I now have a passion for it and I know I will always write to help others, help myself and to be creative. Writing from the heart is powerful and we don't need to be academically gifted to do it (I am certainly not an academic); but I am a person who has a passion for writing and who knows firsthand the benefits of this wonderful divine gift.

Spirit writing

Are you a Spirit Writer? Do you know what a spirit writer is or does?

I know that I am. When I write it is as if I visit another dimension within and writing flows through a different channel than my original thoughts. Strange huh? As I write it is as if I am being guided through the process of what I should put down on that paper or type on the keyboard. The information comes to me at the very moment I need to access it. Unprecedented knowledge invades my thoughts and has to be shared. This is why I call myself a Spirit Writer.

I often comment that I read some of the articles and novels I have written and think, "Wow! Who wrote that?" It is strange but something I embrace because writing fulfils me so much. I learn something from each piece I write and I love to share what it is that I learn about life with others in a hope of creating a more fearless universal understanding of why life is the way it is at times.

When you are connected to your inner spirit you have the ability to write from the heart, not only from a text book. This makes for interesting reading for many genres.

Automatic writing

As the title of this article would be suggestive of channeling I thought I would share some knowledge that I have accessed about the subject of automatic writing (channeling). There is a way of writing that is not of our own which is called Automatic Writing, where the writer states that their writing has been produced from an external/spiritual source without the writer's conscious awareness of the content.

Although I am really intrigued by the work this type of writing produces, I am not saying that I write through spiritual channeling. I write from deep down within where my imagination and accumulated knowledge reside and will only surface for the benefit of my readers. I am sure many writers feel the same.

Writing for expression.

It is well known that people can stay balanced by releasing their innermost thoughts and emotions through the pen. Even if these thoughts are never to be seen by another's eyes, they have been emotionally released.

Have you ever heard the saying, *'A problem shared is a problem halved'*? What if you feel you cannot share your problem with anyone else? A safe alternative is to release it by writing down your emotions. *'A problem written is no longer hidden'*. Maybe through articulating a poem or simply by taking a moment to write down how you feel about what has occurred and how you could possibly resolve the situation will help.

Writing it all down allows you to see it more clearly, give yourself the gift of a new perspective. If you don't have the courage to say to someone what you feel, you could express yourself by sharing your written words. If you don't want anyone else to see what you have written it may be best to dispose of it. You will have already released your thoughts and so healing will have commenced.

Write through your inner spirit and you will write the best that you can possibly write, which is from your heart.

Do you dream of writing?

For me discovering writing has been a poignant moment in my life. I suppose looking back I have always had an interest in writing but never thought it was an option for me as I was not the best at English in school. I always had the dream but I didn't actively have the belief in myself that I could succeed.

It was only when I realised that I was living my dream by actively pursuing writing and allowing my own voice to shine through that my writing flowed freely. I had no expectations of myself other than to explore the passion that was igniting inside of me. I have discovered through writing that I can heal myself because I release pent up emotion through the words I type. It can also be used as a highly effective means of self-expression. I have also discovered that I am motivated to educate myself on numerous subjects and have a desire to share my interpretation of these findings through articles.

The main writing dream of mine was to write a novel. When I embarked on this journey I didn't know how it was going to happen, I just knew that it was time and with a little focus, commitment and a daily word count target I succeeded. It was one of those cases of having a book in me that just flowed out. It was through the belief that I felt from others that I steamed ahead and I will always be grateful for that. So because of this I will always recommend that any new writer shares their writing in a positive, constructive environment so that any feedback is conveyed with the right intention.

From that point onwards I have had a writing bug. I know I will be a writer for the rest of my days. After many years of not knowing what it is that makes me tick, I now know. Writing makes my heart sing and I know that only good will ever come from my writing because I pursue it with the purest of intentions. Writing is the vehicle I utilise to connect and help others.

No two writers are the same. We all write differently even if we are in the same genre so every author is equally unique. However, we are not all equally successful but that is determined on how you measure success. Is being a successful writer selling a million copies of a book? Or getting a million hits for an article? That is up to each individual but for me I know that I am a successful author because I am fulfilled. I am doing exactly what I want to be doing, which is writing to help others learn more about themselves, more about others, offer some alternative thoughts and provide a comforting hug through my thoughts and experiences.

Do you ever dream of writing? Why? Whatever your reason, do it for you. Do it because it makes your heart sing. Do it your way. Always believe in yourself, write about what you believe in and share it with those who believe in you. There are readers for every topic in the world out there ready to read YOUR writing. They will find you but you need to get your work out there first.

Happy writing

* If you are a writer who would like to explore your writing further you are welcome to enquire about publishing your work at adoptamum.com We would love to hear your ideas and we support new writers.

Also why not consider our NOVEL IDEA write a novel program http://www.adoptamum.com/index.php?option=com_k2&;view=item&id=267:novel-idea-write-a-book-mentoring&Itemid=135

How did writing find you?

Anyone who writes knows every writing journey is unique. There are people who do it for a job through journalism and other mediums. There are those of us who do it for self- expression. We use it as a tool to express all of those thoughts that get built up inside and don't get released very often. Some are lucky enough to have their passion rewarded by financial recognition, but mostly we keep at it because it feels right. We get rewarded by the buzz we feel when putting a piece together.

My writing journey was a strange one. I feel like I had an epiphany. The missing piece of my puzzle of life that I searched long and hard for during many years was actually within me all along. It was just not the right time for it to come out. I never thought for one minute during my life before the big 30 that I would ever be a writer. I spent all of my twenties chasing something; I never knew what it was but it was something. I explored theatre but one problem was, I don't have a good memory and remembering lines was a bit of a nightmare. I did enjoy acting though as it gave me a buzz. It ended after my first real performance. I was playing one of the leads in a play called *Lipstick, Powder and Politics* based on young people growing up in the troubles in Northern Ireland. It was really well received and so it was decided it would tour. Alas, for me that would not be the case, I had discovered I was pregnant and it wasn't a look my character would carry off well. I wasn't too downhearted though. I believed it was a sign from the universe that acting was not for me and so I started teaching it instead.

When I moved to Australia from Ireland, something happened. I have heard it said since that Australia is an inspirational place to be and I truly believe it. There are so many wonderfully talented and creative people everywhere you turn, it is truly amazing. I started becoming deeply inspired after having my third child. Within weeks I felt an insatiable urge to write fun learning children's books. I then started to illustrate them. I was expressing creativity in ways that I never imagined I could or even would. I never thought of myself as much of writer or artist and I don't think anyone close to me did either. In fact I always averaged a C grade in English and the best I ever did at art was one A in my first year of secondary school for drawing a rabbit.

After having my fourth child, I was drawn towards more writing for my own genre. The opportunity found me to complete *Nanowrimo,* a yearly challenge to write a novel during November. I did this whilst I breastfed my four-week-old daughter. Shortly after writing *The Visitor*, I was lucky that the opportunity found me to publish it. I have not stopped writing since and I am preparing myself for the challenge again this year.

What type of writer am I? I have to be honest and say that I explore every lane of the spaghetti junction that is my writing journey. Since I began writing I have written and illustrated more than thirty books for my children. I have written and published three novels. I have written many short stories and published more than forty articles. I am no Mia Freedman or JK Rowling yet but you never know, maybe someday. I am always learning and that is what makes it interesting. I like to share what I learn along the way and people appreciate my work, so what more can I ask? I know I will be writing for the rest of my days, I am totally fulfilled because of it.

For anyone contemplating exploring their writing journey, prepare yourself for many detours along the way and brace yourself to find hidden personal depths. My advice would be to listen to your instincts. Write from your heart. Always believe. Never give up. Find a good writing balance that fits well into your life because then you will have a better chance to stick with it. And most important of all, enjoy it!

Writing

"Writing is an exploration. You start from nothing and learn as you go." EL Doctorow.

Many people think of writing as something they would like to do but don't feel they can. I just started at a point and worked to a higher level that I felt comfortable with. I think it has a lot to do with inhibitions. A lot of writing is expressive and there is a chance you are revealing yourself a little bit every time you write. Once this paranoia is in check then writing is a lot easier and has the potential to keep you sane.

By writing you are releasing thoughts and emotions.

Did you know that suppressing thoughts and emotions can be harmful to your emotional welfare? If on the other hand emotions are expressed aggressively to an unsuspecting victim, this can be damaging to you and your relationship with that person and those who care about them. Writing can be a safe and effective way to release.

Starting point

I initially started writing as part of a home study writing course which I have been completing with The Writers' Bureau and I have learned a lot of tips and advice through this course. I did not know how I wanted to write… novels, articles, short stories, journalism, poems. I just knew that I wanted to write. I had a desire, passion and an open mind which got me started and has kept me interested. There is always something new to learn and write about. Everyone will have their own interests and their own starting point.

Individual journey

I look back on my journey as a writer and think about where I am now. How far I have come but also how far I have yet to go - it is all very exciting. I did believe in myself that yes, something could come out of my writing but I never knew how that was going to happen. I feel that I write for the right reasons, which are because I enjoy sharing my thoughts and the things I learn with others. Everyone has their own reasons for writing and each reason is valid.

Advice

My advice to any budding writer is this: When you start writing, share your work with people who will give you positive encouragement and feedback as this will give you the motivation to keep writing. I have been fortunate to have been able to share my work on adoptamum.com since I began writing and my writing has progressed to a level that I am now happy and confident with; I feel lucky to have had this opportunity. There are many places available where you can submit work for publication when you feel comfortable enough to do so. I know mamamia.com accepts submissions from writers, which will give you a great stepping stone up to being an established writer.

Writing tips

- Determine why you want to write. Is it to make money instantly or is it for pleasure?
- Set aside a regular time to write.
- Set goals and challenge yourself.
- Use your heart as guide, connect within.
- Trust in your ability.
- Don't think too much towards the final result, take each step as it comes and you will soon walk that mile.
- Write about things that interest you or that you know a lot about already.
- Write with passion.
- Be selective in your content, present interesting facts, stories or a different perspective.
- Know when you have written too much or not enough.

Articles need to have a balance of facts and a new perspective on the subject you are writing about. I write based on a 3C principle that I created - Clear, Concise and Connect.

It takes a lot of information and preparation to write a book. I can only advise to do your research and familiarise yourself with it. You need to believe what you are writing to enable you to paint the picture, set the scene and convince your readers to believe in your words.

Poems

Poems are all about passion, emotion and experience and are a great tool to connect with others in a deep, meaningful way. When I write a poem I have the core subject matter and I allow ideas to branch from that whilst also connecting with the emotions I would like to project.

Writing about yourself and your experiences can be very helpful in getting your thoughts and emotions out of your head and onto paper, which may help you look at things in a more focused way. We all have a personal journey with challenges and joys that we may or may not want to share with others, but it is the writing and sharing it with ourselves that I feel helps maintain a healthy mind, especially during times of grief or uncertainty. No matter why you choose to write, always be true to yourself and listen to your inner guide as I have discovered this is my best mentor. It is worth noting that as a writer there are no rules. Every writer has their own style and way of doing things and that is good because creative freedom is a must for any budding writer as you explore the fabulous adventure that is writing.

Accidental Publisher

Looking at my background, publishing books would not have been foreseen in my future. Mind you nobody could ever have dared to imagine what I would end up doing as I have always been someone who embraced opportunity and was always 'going somewhere'. I suppose I have always prepared myself to go that little bit further than anyone else. This has often gotten me into strife. During my teenage years and even during my twenties I found it hard to settle as I pursued exciting opportunity after exciting opportunity. I didn't often stop to think why, I just knew that I was following my heart and if it felt right I did it. Areas of employment for me ranged from acting on stage, been a presenter, administration, managing a deli, supervising a high risk area in a meat factory and been a tutor to special needs students in the mental health sector, the list goes on and on and on....

Early Days

I was never good in school; I went to an all girls convent secondary school in Ireland. I remember my parents being so proud that I had passed the entrance exam and earned my place in the most prestigious girls' school in our county. I was very proud too. I was doing well and getting by but I always found it hard in the classes to hold my interest and I would get bored. I know now that I had made the wrong subject choices. Physics would have been a wonderful science to have under my belt but I never thought that I was smart enough to choose it and so I chose biology like my closer peers, mistake!! Looking back now I would have benefited by being more philosophical based in my choices; mind you choices were limited as most of the subjects were compulsory.

To cut a long story short my interests navigated more towards the social side of school and I would often wag school. At recess and lunch I would be found smoking behind the demountable, cigarettes I got from selling my dinner tickets.

I rolled my skirt up high and was I was becoming popular. I liked it, it made me feel good. Said skirt heightening would of course not take place until I was clearly out of view from both home and school.

Not so long ago an old friend from school contacted me on facebook and said *"Imagine if Mr Jones knew that you published your own book"* Mr Jones was my English teacher, he was short with brown hair and eyes and he had two suits which he alternated, one was brown with a lighter brown shirt and a darker brown tie, the other was blue with a blue shirt and a darker blue tie and he had such confidence in himself. He used to make me read out loud in class and it was something I had stayed back after class the day before and asked him not to do because it made me blush excessively and my mind would go in a tizzy. But he made me anyway and I got up and walked out of the class. That rebellious naure was something was not toerated do in this school. But it was definitely the beginning of the demise of my educational prospects in secondary school. I couldn't wait to leave until I got a job and started earning money and that is exactly what I did. I got a job in a tights factory checking stockings for holes. It wasn't glamorous but I thought that I was the bee's knees earning 62 pounds a week. It didn't last long as the company went into administration (maybe they were paying employees too much!!) I got a job in my local town in the meat factory. This was my first experience of feeling that that I was an integral part of a team I loved it, even though the job itself was totally mundane and mind numbing at times the fun we had as a team and the comradery that was connected to it was what made me clock in every day.

Education

When my son was ready to start school I knew that I couldn't do shift work because lifting him out of bed early on a Irish winter morning was not something that I was prepared to do so I resigned from my supervisory position and went back to school. I worked part-time whilst doing an access course which earned me acceptance for a place studying media at university but it was not the right time and I had secured myself a perfect administration job that I was to find out that I enjoyed a lot and that would open doors for me that surpassed any expectation I could of imagined.

I chose to study Humanities through an outreach university programme at my local college and I worked hard juggling everything for a few years.

My manager brought to my attention a course that was available through a Dublin college that would require me to attend a weekend workshop in various locations around

Ireland for the duration of a year. It was fully funded because it was aimed at training people to go out into the community and break down barriers that had been built up during the troubles in Northern Ireland. I was accepted and oh boy did I learn so much during this time!

I was then offered a position teaching with a local college in their out centres, it was perfect and the same year I graduated with a Diploma in Humanities through the University of Ulster. I felt like the luckiest woman in the world and I was!

Turnaround

I endured a low time in my life that navigated me to look inside. This was something I had never even considered when I was rallying through life at an excessive speed. Everything slowed down and simplified around me, it had to or I couldn't have handled it. Luckily I had worked in the mental health sector, and although I was not a nurse I knew what was happening to my mind and I also knew what I needed to do to get through it, I suppose the main thing was not to fear it! I took each day as it came and focused on my children who needed me. I found that this time was invaluable to me in my transition to a more aware person. I looked within and began to see the real Karen that was patiently waiting to make an appearance. I discovered that when we are at a low point it often guides us to a state of contemplation and a more quiet place where the craziness of before is past and with a clear mind positive change can be worked towards.

Discovering creativity

With my new found appreciation for life I ventured forward at a slower pace. Focusing purely on the simple things guided by my heart. We moved to Australia (when I was 35 weeks pregnant with my third child) to set up a new life for our family and when I arrived I felt so inspired. I began writing and illustrating children's books, it made my heart sing and my children loved it. I felt as if my puzzle was coming back together again. I was willing to be patient and go with it, not forcing it like I would have before.

> *"Life is not about finding yourself,*
> *it is about creating yourself"*

I suppose without even knowing it I was re-inventing myself. My son helped me choose the logo Mamma Macs and I began to make the stories into homemade books. Even though this was not about achievement I decided to send my manuscript to a manuscript assessor called Angel Wings Manuscript assessment that was based in Melbourne. When the assessment came back it was so encouraging, it was a great feeling. I didn't do anything with it at that time. I just began to share the love of my stories with my new Australian friend and her beautiful girls; she was always so positive when she spoke of my stories and I even created characters for her girls. As I couldn't afford to send presents to nieces and nephews I would create a character for them, write them a story and do illustrations in their own personal book. As I grew I would computerise the books more. I remember the excitement when I discovered Microsoft Publisher; I could really bring my books to life. When my children were asleep I would sit with my Faber Castell pencils and illustrate pictures for my next book project, I felt free and happy when I did this and seeing my son's face when I produced a new book for him was all of the motivation I needed to keep going. I worked on about 30 books over this period in my life.

My husband seen my passion and wanted to support me as he believed in me so when I seen an advertisement in the paper stating 'Do you want to publish your book, call us' I did. We went to meet the guy in a coffee shop in Applecross (a fancy suburb in Perth, Western Australia). We had arrived early and so took a walk along the water's edge with our kids. I remember mentioning to him that if this guy was a rip off I would be able to do it myself someway. So off we went to meet him and he was charming, of course, and to an enthusiastic aspiring author what he had to offer was priceless, my book published and 500 copies to sell. The approx price he gave me was $8000 and he had papers for me to sign there and then. But something told me not to, it was too much money for my family at the time but I felt that I was wiser for meeting with this guy. It was part of my journey.

I secured a deal with a local children's charity to raise money through the sale of my books, they believed in me and said yes to me putting their name on my books. This was an amazing affirmation for me that others believed in my dream, but time and circumstance didn't align and so I didn't pursue it further. I decided to send my manuscript off to be considered by publishers. I collected a list of submission offices in Australia and I sent my books everywhere. This process takes a very long time and I learned to be patient though my excitement. I was very close to an offer of publication with a few of my manuscripts and so I knew that what I was writing was good. Some of the letters I received came with a personal message expressing that the editors loved my work but that it just didn't fit with their requirements at that time but to please keep submitting.

Passion for writing

I then joined a site called buildingbeautifulbonds.com which was created by my beautiful friend. As I was living away from my mum I thought that I would join. WOW! I was introduced to a more loving metaphysical way of thinking, all of the women on the site shared support and love with one another, it was a virtual sanctuary where we would meet and message each other and we never felt alone. I began to write little things and post them in the groups. I began to write articles on things that inspired me at any given time. I was changing so much at this time and I was absorbing information to support my new found need for information. I showed some of them to the owner of the site and she was excited and asked if I would like to publish them on the site. They flowed and flowed and the owner published them and published them. I was soon offered the position of 'Resident Writer'. This blew my mind! I was so excited; I couldn't believe that I was classed as a writer, someone who had walked out of her English class. I was given up on and I suppose I had given up on myself in that sense but now..... I had found a burning desire to write, write, write and I discovered that as I wrote I healed a little more.

Alignment

When everything shifts and aligns to make something possible it is quite magical and this is what happened when I chose to write my first novel. I had just given birth to my forth child and was feeling very inspired. I had been becoming increasingly aware of the signals we are sent from time to time affirming that we are doing the right thing for us. I came across a writing challenge called Nanowrimo that intrigued me, I had always been a person who excelled when challenged but I hadn't challenged myself in this way for a long time. The urge was there though and although many people would have commented that my timing was not great as I had a new born I knew that the timing was perfect, I was at home and hey what else would I be doing whilst breastfeeding!!
What would I write about? The challenge was starting in a few days and I knew that I had to do it but was I being silly even considering it with only a few days to go? Then it happened. I was watching a bit of morning TV (something that I never did) and Whoopi Goldberg said something that resonated with me so deeply. You see I had experienced a miscarriage a few years previously that

I had not fully healed from. When she mentioned that it had been a visitor that came to help shift me back onto the right track in preparation for receiving the real gift. A truly big AH HA moment for me and I felt an overwhelming urge to share this message with the world, but how? Then I remembered Nanowrimo and I knew that it would happen and it did. For 30 days I wrote 1667 words to achieve the 50000 words required to win the challenge. I could not believe how it all flowed together. Every night the kids would go to bed easily and I would sit with my new born breastfeed her to sleep with one arm and single handed I typed my way to 50000 words. The novel was finished, it was an emotional rollercoaster but I DID IT! What now?

My first publishing experience

Ok so what now? Will I send it to an array of publishers like I did with my children's manuscripts? That didn't sit well with me because I really wanted to bring it to the world now and I didn't want to wait years to have my book in my hand. I shared it with the people I love to get some feedback. My mum is my biggest critique and she absolutely loved it and my closest friend said that it 'Just had to be published'. Then it happened, the site which I was writing for sponsored the publication of my book, how lucky was I? My dream was becoming a reality!!!

I sent a self publishing company my manuscript and the wheels were set in motion. I knew what I wanted for a cover but they told me that the final decision was with them as they knew best. I thought that this was strange. All was sailing along wonderfully, then I got calls from another department of the publishing house wanting me to get my book edited and it was going to cost more than the publication did. This was a whopper, a total dream zapper. So how was this going to happen?, I wanted the best for my book but I didn't want it to be changed I loved my characters and their journeys, but I couldn't have it going out there with my name on it if it wasn't good enough to be read! After much deliberation, and the support of my hard working hubby, I chose to have it edited. To be honest I was surprised at it, I thought that they would have changed heaps of it but they didn't, the lady just gently made it more readable.

The publishing company made a booboo and sent the unedited version to eBook format and I received an email from someone who bought it saying that they found it hard to read and were finding it even harder to get any satisfactory response from the publisher. I contacted the publisher directly and they were not all that helpful at all and would not recognise any blame on their behalf. I asked them to reimburse the lady her money and offer her a free copy of the edited book. I still to this day don't know if they did that. They also wanted to charge me extra for different things and I felt it was becoming a real money pit; they didn't care about me or my book! I would receive phone call after phone call looking for me to buy more books at a 'special price', marketing plans at a 'special price' and it went on and on, I received my first royalty letter stating I had sold an amazing amount of five books and they had earned more royalties on each of these books than I did. It all just seemed so WRONG!

The Publishing venture

But as my quote said in the front of my book 'From all negative situations is the potential for a positive outcome" I chose to focus on the positives I could do with my book. I entered it into the Readers' Favorite book awards contest. It received a 5 star review and was a finalist in the 2012 awards contest. I built up a rapport with the guys at Readers' favourite because I believe so much in them, they work tirelessly and I know that they give more than they receive, they do their job for the love of helping authors move forward in their career by making the process easier. They offer heaps of services from proofreading, to reviewing; to book trailers etc.... the list is endless.

I had since also completed my second novel and things were exciting for me as an author. I noticed that affirmations were coming from all around letting me know I was doing the right thing. Being an author and selling books can be a full time job so I researched what works and what doesn't and began to identify who was real and who wasn't. There are many people out there in the writing business who give more than they take in financial gain; to have a connection with people like this is priceless!

One of my friends from Buildingbeautifulbonds.com approached me early 2011 and asked if I thought that it would be possible to publish books. She was a fan of my work and I had mentored her to write her life story '*In Search of My Soul*'. I had a think about it and after some research I discovered that everything that the publishing company I hired to publish my book used services that I could utilise myself and I could have complete control of my own book and royalties. Instead of earning $2 a book commission I could print my book for $4 to $5 and keep the rest for myself.

After a lot of work and research I worked it all out. I discovered that the US based Ingram Company Lightning Source had recently set up an office in Melbourne (Time + Circumstance = Magic). I felt that I had nothing to lose and so I applied to Lightning Source to open a publishing account as a publisher. This was what we needed as it provided us with access to worldwide distribution and we could print as little or as many books as we wanted. We could also place orders for overseas orders by using their printing houses in both the UK and the US.

We got accepted as a publisher and we affiliated with Buildingbeautifulbonds.com who supported us and believed in us so much. As soon as we put up our logo a book submission came through with a truly inspirational story. Our vision was to publish inspirational stories so we had it edited and published Prickle in a Dream within a month and have not stopped since.

Guided

From the offset I was guided through each step of the way. If I had of thought of the every step as a whole picture we would have been totally overwhelmed and ran away. Instead I chose to take one step at a time and every challenge was an opportunity to learn and grow and oh boy I love to learn new things.

I discovered my absolute passion for creating books. When one of our authors sends me a signed copy of their book thanking me for helping them make their dream come a reality I beam with immense joy that I have been a positive influence on their publishing journey

Little achievements would come along at exactly the right time to affirm that I was on the right path with Serenity Press. A few of these to date are:
- In 2012 I was awarded acceptance into Stanford's Who's Who.
- In 2013 I was asked to be part of my first Perth based weekend conference.
- In 2014 We were accepted as a publisher by APA.
- In 2014 we begin our transition to becoming a traditional publisher.
- In 2015 I was a finalist in the Business Excellence category of Ausmumpreneur.
- In 2015 the wonderful Monique Mulligan joined our team, her expertise is exceptional.
- In 2015 we had the most successful launch of our first Romance antholgy Rocky Romance at the inaugural Rockingham Book Fair.
- In 2015 we were given permission to gift Oprah a Serenity Press gift basket when she came to visit.

- In 2016 I became an Ausmumpreneur Writing an Publishing expert.
- In 2016 we had the most amazing authors submit for our Writing the Dream anthology.
- We have secured links with an into store distributor.
- We will continue to grow, think outside the box, support Australian authors and grow a strong Serenity Press team.

Attraction

I know that I have utilised the universal Law of Attraction to bring to me exactly what it is that I want to experience in my lifetime. I am so convinced that we all have the power to create and thing that we want into our lives and when we connect this power to following our hearts desire magic will happen! I decided to put my study cap on again and I earned myself a certification as an advanced Law of Attraction Practitioner I have learned that we are the only ones who limit ourselves. I apply this to my business principle and it allows for Serenity Press to grow, albeit unconventionally, but most definitely with passion and determination.

"Where there is a will there is always a way."

I have always lived by this motto and now with my new found appreciation for life I utilise it to be the best I can possibly be!

Conclusion

The Serenity Press initial vision was to share as many inspirational stories with the world as we possibly can but this has been further enhanced by offering authors the opportunity to publish their books in a positive way. I am passionate that our authors will never feel negative about their book. Your book publishing experience deserves to be a positive one.

I have always known that Serenity Press would be an inspirational story in itself; I know this because we have the truest of intention with every endeavour we undertake. We have made affiliations with wonderful people and the only way is up for us. We are a publisher with heart and as we grow our authors grow too. We are a family and I am proud of what we continually achieve with our wonderful authors.

This book was written from a period between 2008 and 2014.

About K P Weaver

Karen is a heart writer who embraces the beauty in every day and hopes to share that with others through her writing. She embraced her passion for writing when she moved from Ireland to Australia in 2008. Karen writes romance, spiritual, self-help and children's books.

She has a diploma in humanities and with a background of tutoring drama to special needs students she hopes to continue to be a positive part of people's lives.

Karen is the proud founder of Serenity Press, MMH Press and the Everything Publishing Academy.

She lives close to the beach in Waikiki, Western Australia with all of her six children close by.

You can find Karen on social media and at
www.serenitypress.org
www.mmhpress.com

Books by K P Weaver

FICTION
The Visitor
The Wish Giver
The Memory Taker

Outback Dancer (coming soon)
The Stamp Collector (coming soon)
The Lighthouse Keeper (coming soon)

NOVELETTES
Beached
The Darkest Ocean
Forbidden Love

NON FICTION
The Magic in Mindfulness
The Power of Knowing
The Miracle of Intention
The Law of Love
The Gift in Gratitude
The Alchemy of Life Magic
Everything Publishing

CHILDREN'S BOOKS

Australian Animal Walkabout
Bumble Bee Rock Around the Clock
Roly Poly Rainbow Princess
Irish Dancing Girl
Alphabet Job Buddies
Minky Monkey meets (26 book series)
Mommy Monster says (6 book series)

Lightning Source UK Ltd.
Milton Keynes UK
UKHW011040170121
377131UK00001B/3